# Seeking Common Bonds

# Seeking Common Bonds

33 Ways to Build Affinity and Strengthen Relationships

BETSY A. ROZELLE

ISBN-13: 9781981552825
ISBN-10: 1981552820

# Contents

# Acknowledgments

**THANK YOU!**

THIS BOOK IS finally finished because of those who encouraged me and gave constructive feedback throughout the process. Thank you SO MUCH to Bree Talbot (my lovely daughter and best cheerleader), Trish Propson (who lent her considerable talents to the cover design and graphics), Mary McNevin, Jeff Hayes, Kathy Westover, Colleen Maxey, Nicole McNevin, Dawn Giesen, and all those who encouraged me and prayed. Thanks also to Kathi Bloy, my editor; I'd highly recommend her.

My husband, Ben, is not much of a reader (unless it's hunting or wildlife related), so when he surprised me with "I might even read your book when it's finished," I took that as a sign of encouragement.

Finally, and not any less importantly, thank *you* for taking the time to read this book! My sincere hope is that you become more intentional about seeking common bonds with people. May the word "affinity" become an integral part of your vocabulary … and your life.

# Dedication

*My daughter and son-in-law are expecting their first baby (a girl!) – my first grandchild! The baby and this book are due to come out at about the same time. Needless to say, 2018 is going to be quite an exciting year. I dedicate this book to my granddaughter and any future grandchildren, with the hope that they experience as much joy in life as even the thought of them has already brought to me.*

*-BETSY ROZELLE*

---

*"What a thought-provoking book! I've already envisioned several ways that Betsy's Affinity- Building training and her action steps can help build cohesion in our work groups. I'm so aware now of affinity-building opportunities and how to use them as a foundation for better relationship building."*

*--COLLEEN RICHESON MAXEY, VICE PRESIDENT SALES &*
*MARKETING, JACK RICHESON & CO.*

# 1

## Affinity: What The Heck Is It?

*The common bond of humanity and decency that we share is stronger than any conflict, any adversity, any challenge.*

–WES MOORE, AMERICAN AUTHOR AND
DECORATED US ARMY OFFICER

**Affinity**
My definition:
The bond or connection between and among people, based on common experiences, passions, and interests. The ability to discover and develop those bonds is the key to successful relationship building.

**Affinity**
Merriam Webster's simple definition:
A feeling of closeness and understanding that someone has for another person because of their similar qualities, ideas, or interests; a liking for or an attraction to something; a quality that makes people or things suited to each other

**Affinity Synonyms:**
Similarity, resemblance, likeness, empathy, sympathy, fellow feeling, attraction, like-mindedness, rapport, kinship, compatibility, solidarity, same wavelength, fondness, simpatico, common ground, common bond

"On a scale of one to ten, what is your pain?" the OB-GYN nurse asked as I entered another round of contractions.

"About an eight," I grunted, dreading what a ten was going to feel like. Because I had decided months earlier not to use any pain medication or an epidural, I knew I was in for an "interesting" experience.

"OK, let's turn you over on your side so your labor can be more productive," the nurse said.

*More productive* turned out to be *more agonizing* as the pain soon hit a 9.8. They didn't tell us in Lamaze class that you will likely feel like your body is going to snap in half. I suppose there's no way to really explain that type of body contortion. You just have to *feel* it.

That's how it is with pain. You just have to feel it to understand it.

My nurse used the one-to-ten scale so that she and I would have some basis of comparison. Compared to other pain I've felt in my life, how bad was my contraction? Would her number have been the same had she been feeling the same pain? Probably not, but at least she knew how bad *I* thought it was. And, since she had once given birth, she had a fairly good idea of what I was feeling.

Trying to describe pain—like trying to describe a sound, an experience, a smell, a sight, or a taste—requires having a basis for comparison. The person to whom we're describing it must have heard, experienced, smelled, seen, or tasted something similar in the past, or the description won't work. If I tell you that something tastes "really sweet," you have to have experienced a sweet taste to have any idea of what I'm describing. If I tell you that I stubbed my toe really hard or that I burned my finger on a stove burner, you probably can relate to the pain I'm feeling. You've experienced it before.

Have you ever tried to explain what a specific spice tastes like?

Describe the taste of cinnamon.

I can't. It tastes like ... cinnamon. I'd be hard pressed to create a specific enough description to really tell you how it tastes. Unless you've tasted it, you have no idea what it means if someone says, "It tastes like cinnamon."

So it is with most life experiences. Unless you've labored through the unique pain of childbirth, for example, it's hard to imagine the feeling. Unless you've sat on a frigid metal bleacher at Lambeau Field and watched a Packers game, you can't accurately grasp the sights, sounds, smells, and tastes that are involved. Unless you've run a marathon, you can't really understand what it means to "hit the wall." Unless you've gone through a divorce, you can only imagine the trauma. You get the picture.

## So What?

Legendary Green Bay Packers coach Vince Lombardi is famous for reminding his team about the fundamentals. *"Gentlemen, this is a football."*

Most of the soft-skills training you've experienced has a fundamental common denominator: relationship building. Every parenting class, customer service training, sales manual, leadership training, or team building session has an element of "people skill" development. Makes sense, right?

What doesn't make sense is that the trainer usually assumes that all people already know about the basic building blocks of relationship development and how to successfully use those skills. In this book, I don't make that assumption.

All soft-skills training essentials— personal and professional — begin with the need to learn how to build affinity between people. All other skill sets build on those basic principles. You and your team will reach your greatest potential only when you've become proficient at the very basic skill of affinity building.

## Common Experiences

Common experiences of smells, sounds, sights, tastes, and physical pain and pleasure help us to form affinities with other people who've experienced the same things. It's one of the first ways we bond with people.

I weave this concept of affinity building into all of my work and relationships---always looking for common ground. Heading into each new experience with the idea that it will help me relate to people who've had that same experience is invigorating.

I toted a shotgun around the woods with my husband one year during grouse hunting season just to gain an understanding of why he was passionate about the sport (oh, and because I had lost a weight-loss bet with him). I get it now. I'll never be a good shot, and I may never hunt again, but now I understand why he enjoys it so much. Not only did I enjoy the training of target shooting—I'm much better at hitting a stationary bullseye than a creature that moves—but I appreciated the challenge of improving each time I pulled the trigger. The bruise on my shoulder indicated that I was a real "lightweight" and first-time shooter, but that didn't stop me from wanting to keep shooting. When I donned my father-in-law's hunting vest and my hiking boots on the morning of the hunt, I could smell the anticipation in the woods. With each step we took, my heart beat a bit faster. What I didn't anticipate is how darn fast and sneaky those grouse would be. Ben's "shoot from the hip" method was fun to watch. I loved how we had to communicate non-verbally as we navigated the thick woods, and I felt and saw each shade of green from a new perspective. The fact that I shot zero grouse didn't prevent me from finally understanding the allure of the hunt.

With EVERY SINGLE PERSON in the world, you have several things in common. Some of those things may be obvious—eye color, nationality, stature--- and some are much less visible—passion for a specific hobby, spiritual beliefs, past hurts.

## The Venn Diagram

Remember Venn diagrams from elementary school? They were usually used in math class but, don't worry, there's no math in this book ... just the basic principal of intersections.

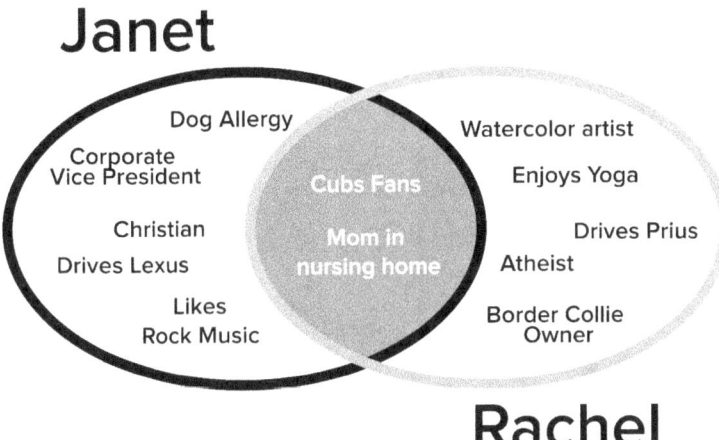

This Venn diagram represents two of my fictitious friends. The left circle is Janet, the VP of Human Resources at a large paper products company. She's a devout Christian, drives a Lexus, listens to rock music, and is severely allergic to dogs. Rachel, the right circle, is my free-spirited friend who practices yoga, is a Prius-driving liberal atheist, proud owner of a border collie, and makes her living as a watercolor artist. If you look at the descriptors in the outer edges of the circle, it appears that Janet and Rachel don't have a lot in common on the surface. However, the descriptors in the intersection are pretty strong affinities that could be used to "strike a common chord." Can you imagine the joy that both of them felt when the Cubs finally made it all the way? Do you think if Janet and Rachel were in the dining area of a nursing home helping their respective moms eat dinner, they would find a connection that would transcend the world of music or organized religion? I think so.

Is it impossible to build a relationship if there are no descriptors in the intersection? No, but it sure is easier to begin a conversation about something both individuals have in common.

Wouldn't it be interesting to have each member of the United States Congress fill out a Venn diagram with a member of the opposite party? I daresay there would be some very important commonalities in the intersections upon which some civil relationships could be built.

Take, for example, the issue of the controversial protests ("taking a knee") of some NFL players during the national anthem. Your friends and family may be divided on how they feel about this. Here's a Venn loosely based on two people I know:

If James and Tony never get to know each other outside of a political discussion, they would probably not feel much affinity for each other; in fact, they may not even like each other. But if they dig deeper to learn more about each other, they'll discover some pretty important commonalities. Think of the difference it could make when they learn they both have sons overseas in the military. Might it be possible they could even strike up a conversation about their last scuba-diving experience?

Will James and Tony change their respective opinions about the NFL player protests if they complete this Venn diagram exercise? Probably not. But, what will hopefully change is their level of understanding and respect for each other. They'll get to know each other as men instead of just as opponents in a heated discussion.

## What do We have in Common?

Here's a simple exercise to illustrate how many things you and I have in common. It's important to note that affinity building is also learning about things you *don't* have in common.

Read these random facts about me:

1. I sang bass in a girls' barbershop quartet, and I'm now usually the voice singing an octave lower than the rest of the women.
2. I was adopted when I was 2 years old. My name was then changed from Joy Marie to Betsy Ann.
3. I love pasta—too much.
4. I am a Christian. I believe that Jesus Christ is my Lord and Savior and the only reason I'm going to heaven. I want EVERYONE to know the saving love and grace of Jesus.
5. I was a straight-A student in my small-town high school. Does that mean I'm smart? Nope. It just means I was good at doing school.
6. A member of my family died of an accidental heroin overdose.
7. I love the cartoons in *The New Yorker,* especially the "contest" ones in the back. On my bucket list is "have one of my cartoon captions be a finalist in a *New Yorker* contest."
8. I know the ugly pain of divorce ... but I also know the joy of new beginnings.
9. I've run (albeit slowly) two half marathons.
10. I'm addicted to online word games, and I love good puns (because that's how eye roll).
11. I love rummage sales, thrift shops, and clearance racks. Much to my husband's chagrin, one of my favorite hang-outs

is the Goodwill Outlet (yes, there IS such a thing, usually only one in each state).

12. One of my favorite places in the world is Tuscany, and not just because of #3.

13. My husband is an avid deer hunter ... I've learned to like venison.

14. I enjoy reading legal thrillers, mystery and suspense novels, and historical fiction. And, for those who haven't read all of Lee Child's "Jack Reacher" books, Jack doesn't look anything like Tom Cruise ... just so you know.

15. My first job out of college was at a chamber of commerce. I spent some time in sales, was an executive director for a non-profit agency, and oversaw grantmaking at a community foundation.

Is there at least one fact that "strikes a chord" with you, or that you can "relate to"? Is there a fact that makes you want to share something about yourself with me or ask me questions? Interestingly, when I read a list of facts about people, it is often something I *don't* have in common with them that I find most intriguing. In any case, the exchange of information about ourselves is the key to affinity building.

Your relationship with other people isn't about what hobbies you like, your favorite authors, or the best vacations you've ever had. But it is about why all of those experiences and passions matter. It's about connecting to other people through those affinities, those commonalities. This connection makes the things you don't have in common that much more interesting and important.

I ran into an old friend several years ago after not having seen her for several years. We had both since been divorced and remarried. When we embraced, she whispered, "We have a new affinity." Immediately these new life experiences, albeit painful, created a new bond between us. That word *affinity* stuck with me for a long time, stuck to the point of making it a central theme of this book and my professional focus. I began thinking of how rich my life is because of how wide my affinity circle has become, and how many experiences—positive, negative, and neutral—have built links to others who have "been there."

My theory about affinity and its importance stems from watching it in action over several years and paying attention to the role it plays in human interaction. At various workplaces I noticed that some work teams weren't effective largely because the manager didn't work to build affinity with his/her team members. Some neighborhoods I lived in were more "bonded" than others. Some churches I attended felt aloof; others felt closely-knit.

As I observed and explored, I saw that the key to effective relationships between and among people is the intentional action of finding commonalities and building upon them. The foundation of that affinity building is, of course, love and caring.

**IMPORTANT TO NOTE:** Before you read on, let me acknowledge what probably has already become obvious. You and I may be very different from each other. There are parts about me you may not like or appreciate. That's OK. Truly it is. You will learn a lot about me because affinity building includes sharing about yourself so that others can find commonalities and bonds. Thank you in advance for allowing me to intersect with you through the pages of this book. Ideally we will meet online or in person in the future to seek common bonds.

Explore with me, and be open to developing – first in your mind, then in your daily life – enhanced relationships built on affinities with others.

# 2

---

## How Does This Affinity Thing Work?

*Am I not destroying my enemies when I make friends of them?*

– ABRAHAM LINCOLN

F YOU, LIKE me, flip through a non-fiction book to pick and choose which parts to read, BE SURE TO READ THIS CHAPTER. This is the Affinity Building 101 of the book.

None of the definitions or examples of affinity matters if we're not intentional about building affinities. Some of us find it very natural to build relationships with people; others need to work harder at it. Either way, it requires practice. Scattered throughout this book, you will find action items. Become an intentional affinity builder by *doing* these things on a regular basis. Some will seem elementary; some may be out of your comfort zone. Like any skill, affinity building requires practice. Consider the action items part of your practice routine.

 ACTION

| Ask questions! |
| --- |

One of the best and easiest ways to learn about others and build relationships with them is to ask them questions. Dale Carnegie (*How to Win Friends and Influence People*) and other wise men and women before and after him preach this elementary concept. Want to strike up a conversation with someone new? Ask her how she met her husband; ask her where she got that adorable dress; ask her what she likes best about her job. It doesn't matter ... just show interest in her by asking her *something about herself*.

Most of us are offered connection opportunities on a regular basis. It's how we convert these connections into intersections that helps us build affinity. Let's look at some scenarios, using Abby, who is an intentional affinity builder. What could you say/do in each of the following examples, to build on the affinity that Abby starts?

1    *You meet Abby at a party, and, after chatting about hobbies and interests with you, she says, "Oh, you would love my brother-in-law—he's an avid mountain climber, too."*

2    *Your colleague Abby says to you, "I heard a great speaker at this weekend's conference. She was talking about sleep apnea and I thought of you and your recent diagnosis."*

3    *You're in the checkout line at the grocery store, wearing a tee shirt that sports your alma mater. The woman behind you (Abby) says, "UCLA—cool, I graduated from there in 1979. Did you go there?"*

In each of those examples, Abby deliberately created an intersection and offered you the opportunity to build on it. In the first scenario, you could just nod and smile about Abby's brother-in-law as the conversation turns to other topics. Or you could say, "That's great—does he belong to a club?" or "Does he live around here? I'm always looking for climbing partners." Years later, you may look back and realize that the only reason you met the friend you just climbed Mt. Everest with is that you followed up on a one-sentence opportunity at a cocktail party.

In the second scenario, Abby makes it a point to let you know that she's thinking of you---that's an open door. For you not to invite her to expand on what the speaker said would be a huge missed opportunity. Obvious responses would be, "Did the speaker give any handouts I could look at? I'm trying to gather as much information as possible about all the different technologies out there for apnea." That follow-up question could lead to you finding out about local support groups or chat sites that could open doors to new friendships, new knowledge, and, of course, new affinities.

In the third example, you can enthusiastically let Abby know what your connection is to UCLA. Even if it's the fact that you bought the shirt at a garage sale, you can take advantage of her interest by asking her what her major was.

We are given countless opportunities each day for building affinities. This week listen and watch closely for those cues, and follow up on them by asking questions, showing interest, and intentionally enlarging your intersections.

 ACTION

## SHARE YOUR STORIES!

Imagine how thrilled I was to see the following letter my pastor wrote in our church's November 2017 newsletter. It beautifully illustrates the "why" of affinity building. I always knew Pastor Wade was a great affinity builder, but to see him encourage us with these words really affirmed my passion for deeper relationship building.

## From the Pastor's Desk
### *Ask & Share*

Recently, I had the honor to officiate at the Memorial Service of Karen Lueck. As I talked to the family, I learned that Karen was a competitive dancer. I had no idea! In preparation for her eulogy, I actually did a Google search on her instructor/partner. His name popped up, along with his phone number. I gave him a call and had a wonderful time listening to him recall his experiences with Karen. I was flabbergasted!

Honestly, as I contemplated this incident, I realized I have been to or conducted several memorial services where I learned something about the deceased that I wish I would have known when they were alive. War experiences, hobby interests, adventuresome travels, near death experiences – WAIT, why did I not know this about him or her?!? I pondered the possibility that the fault is mine. I didn't actively nurture the relationship. I didn't ask enough questions, or the right questions.

I always defaulted to conversations about weather, health, sports and religion (I get a free pass to talk about religion, in spite of the taboo of talking about politics and religion). Maybe, I just didn't listen closely enough. But then, the blame could have been theirs! They didn't want to share personal information. They thought no one would care. They were embarrassed about the incident or circumstance.

In my heart, I think everyone has something very interesting to share. Our job is to find out what it is. I have decided that I want to make an effort to make some changes. I am going to try and be more intentional about really getting to know people. I will work to improve my "ask" and my "share". I look at so many bible verses that talk about walking worthy of the calling... being humble, gentle and patient with one another....about counting others more significant than yourselves... about breaking bread together. These cause me to think about the call to love your neighbor as yourself. We can do that more effectively when we ask the right questions and share the right information.

I think all this leads to having more transparent, honest, revealing conversations. This might include interesting or exciting subjects – or it might be about something painful. Either way, we are called to engage, encourage, challenge and exhort one another. That will never happen when we talk about the Packers or the weather.

I sat for a minute and recalled the fact that I know people who: once sold car to Cheap Trick, earned their pilot's license at age 16, crewed a 32' fiberglass jet boat up the Mekong Delta in Vietnam, worked as an avalanche patrolman in Switzerland. And I realized that I have a relationship with each of these people that has allowed me to get way beyond the weather and sports.

I hope you are encouraged to engage the people around you in a way that encourages deep and meaningful conversations. Be prepared for some great surprises and for some deep discussions. Most of all, be prepared to better love your neighbor as yourself.

Go and make disciples,
Pastor Wade

Get beyond the weather and sports with people by sharing your stories and asking about theirs.

You don't need to be a good storyteller to share stories about yourself. When we hear other people talk about their past experiences, it sparks memories in us. The stories don't have to be long and drawn out; often an "I remember one time when I was a kid and my dad brought home our first brand new car ..." type of recollection is all you need to get a great conversation going. Most of us have memories of cars that our families had. The one that sticks out for me is the "Blue Goose," a hideous clunker that my dad drove for work. My first car was a 1979 silver Monte Carlo.

Everyone likes a good story. There are so many benefits to telling things—important or trivial--about ourselves, but some people are either uncomfortable doing it or simply aren't experienced with it. *If you're one of those people, start today by thinking of an interesting or unique thing that you've experienced, and talk about it out loud.* It could be a story about stubbing your toe, getting the wrong food order at a fast-food restaurant, receiving a certain diagnosis from your doctor ... anything. Tell the story to a friend, family member, or even to a complete stranger. Stories matter! When we hear other people talk about themselves, we catch glimpses of ourselves in their lives. You may not be a mountain climber, but if you hear someone talk about what it was like to climb Mount Everest, you can relate to the concepts of pain, challenge, and victory.

Your story can be a couple sentences long and delivered orally, or it can be written and several pages long. The point is to be *transparent* and *intentional* about sharing things about yourself. After hearing or reading your story, people should:

1.  Learn one or more new things about you.
2.  Feel the urge to ask you questions about your story.
3.  Want to share their story with you and/or share their feedback and personal experiences regarding your story.
4.  Want to get to know you better.

Here's a column I wrote for *The Post-Crescent* newspaper a few years back.

*Babysitting and working at the local root beer stand were my first "paying jobs."*

*My first bona fide full-time job, though, came the summer after my high-school graduation when I was 17. The classified ad read, "Be an activist." In 1983, just out of high school, I wasn't that familiar with the term "activist." I had to look it up in the dictionary. The environmental organization touted itself as a citizens' group and was advertising for canvassers. Having done my share of door-to-door canvassing with our local Community Fund, I figured I was qualified. Never mind that my folks were dyed-in-the-wool Republicans who frowned upon all that tree-hugging garbage. I was, after all, a capitalist and needed money for college. If it meant going door-to-door to shut nuclear power plants down, so be it.*

*My parents weren't very enthusiastic about the job opportunity, but they weren't very enthusiastic about any of my choices back then. I was planning to move out of the house into an apartment with a girlfriend, so my incentive to make money grew daily.*

*Coincidentally, one week before my job interview with the organization, a canvasser knocked on my parents' door. He did a real number on Mom, and she coughed up $2.00 (that amount, I later learned, landed her on the "Cheap Sheet," the bottom page of the clipboard that canvassers hide, lest the neighbors get the idea that it's OK to give only $2.00).*

*Listening intently to the canvasser's spiel, I pictured myself doing the same thing. "Is it true," I asked him after letting him know I had applied for a job there, "that you can actually make $200 a week doing this?"*

*"Certainly," Joel replied, not wanting to imply, of course, that he personally was going to be getting a sizable chunk of my mom's less-than-generous donation.*

*I drove past the organization's office a couple times a half hour before my interview, wondering whether this place was really legitimate. Those were pre-internet days when you couldn't just do a Google search.*

*Imagine my surprise as a 17-year-old wet-behind-the-ears small-town girl when I walked into the office and saw that my interviewer was an African American man. I had rarely seen (much less had a conversation with) a black man.*

*The interview was easy. I felt pretty confident that I had what it took. I was offered the job the next day and began the following week. Arthur, the man who interviewed me, was the field manager and my boss. While Arthur was the only man of color in the office, he certainly wasn't the only colorful man (or woman). I felt like a floundering fish in a sea of loose left-wing activists. Nevertheless, we were a family of sorts, "fighting the same fight." Spending several hours a week together in a station wagon bonded us, too. After a while, I got used to the fact that some of the women didn't shave their armpits or wear undergarments.*

*I never got used to the drugs, though. Never in my life had I ever seen anyone (except on TV) use illegal drugs. A couple weeks into the job a bunch of us went across the street before work to have lunch. The group was welcoming back John, a man fresh out of jail for drug possession. Having had my mind stretched a bit during those two weeks around "free thinkers," I was OK having lunch with a former drug user. I was not OK when, halfway through lunch, John dumped a white powder on the table, neatly shaped it into a straight line, rolled a dollar bill, and snorted. I nearly slid under the table, wondering if I could possibly get busted just by sitting with this guy. We weren't busted, but several unsuspecting citizens that day opened their doors to coked-up canvassers.*

*Drugs aside—I tried to stay as far away from them as possible, which wasn't an easy task when the driver of the station wagon was sometimes smoking weed—I was eager to see if I could actually make $200 a week. Minimum wage was $3.35, so clearing $5.00 an hour for just walking* *door-to-door chatting with people sounded like a pretty good deal to me. Well, needless to say, my calculations didn't factor in the variables of a "sales" position like this one—the rejections, the come-ons, the danger of walking around alone carrying money, and the fatigue factor of an outdoor job.*

*Seventeen, with a lot to learn. And learn I did.*

*Even amidst the barking dogs, flirtatious men, lonely housewives, and angry conservatives (including a nuclear power plant worker who chased me down the driveway with a scissors), it was possible to make $200 a week, and much more, for those with the "gift of gab." I'm embarrassed to admit that my average per-hour wage as a 17-year-old canvasser was more than my hourly wage my first year out of college at a chamber of commerce. A lot of folks whose doors we knocked on would ask us how much money we made (which, in theory, they have a right to know, given that it's a "citizens'" group). We were taught to answer that question with, "Our average pay is about minimum wage." That was not true for most of us. We were supposed to take into account the fact that we spent at least ten hours a day "at work."*

*We'd usually arrive around 11:00 a.m., do role playing to practice our "rap," and get assigned our territory for the day. Maps in hand, we'd load into a couple station wagons and head off to save the earth--or make money for college. We'd usually eat lunch together at a restaurant in the town we canvassed. Some days we returned to the office by 8:00 p.m., some days later, depending on the city. Apparently, the stops we made at bars on the way home comprised some of those minimum wage calculated hours. At any rate, I averaged about $450 a week, well above minimum wage at the time.*

*A lot of my door-to-door encounters stick in my mind, but my favorite was the elderly lady on an upscale lake road in Menasha, WI who hobbled to her mansion door with a cane. Hers was my first stop of the day, a day that threatened rain. When I saw the large portrait of Ronald Reagan perched on an easel in the marble-floored foyer, I figured I may as well check this house off my list as a "no, thank you." I was, however,* intrigued by the fact that this family was listed as a "call back," meaning they had made a donation the previous year. While it's not impossible to squeeze a donation to environmental causes from a card-carrying Republican, it's not probable.

I started my "rap" with the typical, "I'm Betsy Reinke from ... we'd like to thank you for your previous support, which allowed us to"…..and then recited the several great things we did with this lady's money the previous year. When she turned toward her elevator to get her checkbook, I threw in the standard, "Anything you'd like to contribute in addition to your membership would really be appreciated ... we're also working on ..."

Relieved that she actually returned with her checkbook, I started in again with a barrage of issues, hoping to hit her hot button. As soon as I mentioned wetlands, her eyes lit up and she said, "Those poor deer, someone has to protect them." As her pen hit her check, I reminded her again how much we'd really appreciate anything in addition to the membership (which was $15.00). Last year she had given $50, which is way above average. Fingers crossed, I held my breath as I watched her write a "2" on the dollar line ... then a "0," so I figured $20 was a good way to start my day. When she wrote the second "0," I thought maybe she had made a mistake ... but, no, she wrote "two hundred and no/100" on the next line. Holy acid-rain-affected mackerel! At 40% commission, I had just made eighty bucks in five minutes ... and I had just begun for the day.

When my field manager picked me up that evening, I was sopping wet, clutching my clipboard close to my body, and beaming from ear-to-ear. I had raised over $1,000 and hardly used any of my territory. In one day, I netted $400 for my college fund, not to mention helped save some wetlands. Not bad for a 17-year-old small-town girl. Capitalism at its finest.

So, let's apply the 4 questions to my story.

1. Did you learn one or more new things about me?
2. Does my story prompt any questions or something further you'd want to discuss?

3. Do you have a story you could share in response (perhaps about an interesting job you've had)?
4. Does my story make you want to get to know me better? Or, perhaps it makes you want to lecture me on the evils or benefits of capitalism.

## How to Share without Bragging: The Christmas Letter Challenge

"But, Betsy," people have lamented, "whenever I talk about myself, I feel like I'm bragging."

If the fear of being viewed as an egotist or braggart is stopping you from talking about yourself, get over it. Unless you're talking about yourself simply to build yourself up or to get attention, there's no reason to worry. Be honest and transparent *for the purpose of building relationships with others.*

Love them or hate them, the annual Christmas letter that is a tradition for some usually gives a wealth of information about the sender. But all too often the letter becomes a bragging expedition. When you're talking about yourself and your family, there's a fine line between boasting and sharing.

I've discovered that humor can go a long way to help fill people in on your life without boring or annoying them. And, if humor isn't your natural bent, you can still take a "light-hearted" approach to talking about yourself and your family. I think you'll learn a lot about my family from our Christmas letter (this one's from 2009) and hopefully see that I'm not intending to brag.

# The Reason Our Family Is Thankful in 2009

10   The 4 of us are healthy and gainfully employed, and for that we're grateful.   Ben is still Zach's boss at Rozelle Construction and is as hard-nosed as ever: "It's not quitting time until I say it's quitting time ... or until the walleye run, grouse, duck, bear, bow hunting, gun-deer hunting, or muzzleloading season starts."   Bree's still full-time with Thrivent Financial and going to college on-line full time.   Betsy still has her freelance writing business and now also works part-time for CAP Services, a community action agency.   By 2012, she'll have 2 years of community organizing under her belt and will be poised to run for U.S. President.   Get your yard signs ready . . .

9   The big hunting news of the year is the bigger-than-average bear Ben shot.   It's amazing how sweet a bear tastes after she's been eating raspberry jam and expired circus peanuts for 3 months.   We're not even close to finishing the venison from the doe Ben shot with his bow and arrow, but that's not discouraging him from sitting for hours in the woods with his muzzleloader to get the buck he was deprived of during the gun hunt.

8   Ben and Betsy had a blast hosting a businessman from India in the U.S. for a Rotary Group Study Exchange with Betsy's Rotary Club.   Our guest, a Hindu vegetarian, didn't complain about sleeping in our guest room next to a big walleye mount and several hunting photos.

7   Zach traded in his old motorcycle for a Honda CBR.   It's painted neon orange ... case the cops can't hear him coming.   In the spirit of supporting the economy, reducing the company's carbon footprint, and getting cash for Rozelle Construction's old beater plow truck, Ben and brother Bard bought a Toyota Prius.   Minutes before taking delivery, the dealer informed them that the government's guidelines wouldn't allow the truck to qualify for buying a Prius. Two days later, Ben drove up in an H3 Hummer, his new "Cash for Clunkers" compromise . . . go figure.

6   Bree's winning performance awards at Thrivent and doing very well in college, but we can't figure out how she passed her math classes, considering she still can't compute the difference between 21 and 20.   She's wondering if she can dip into her 401 (k) to pay underage drinking fines.

5    Ben and Betsy schlepped the obligatory cheese and venison sausage to Maui again for a fun-filled vacation with Harry and Mooie and 14 other relatives.  Ben chose to ignore the age-old warning to never swim in the ocean immediately following a bad storm because the churned water attracts sharks into the shallows.  While snorkeling alone, he nearly became lunch for a shark, oblivious to it until a man on shore started jumping up and down, yelling and making shark signals when he saw the fin just feet from where Ben was.    Visions of a one-armed deer-hunting season flashed through Ben's mind.
In Ft. Lauderdale with Tom, Bre, Uncle Ralph, and Aunt Mary Ellen, Ben and Betsy experienced horse-track betting for the first time.  Using scientific methods such as "Look, that horse just pooped so it's bound to be faster … pick it to win," they managed to lose under $20.00 and have a blast.

4    Cousins' weddings (Patrick/Becky and Grace/Roger) provided great family fun.  While in Chicago, a "free potato pancake" coupon in a hotel flyer led Betsy, Ben, Tom, and Bre to Manny's, Barack Obama's favorite deli.  A Seinfeld-episode-worthy situation ensued, as the smooth-running routine of the deli-line was thrown off by the coupon.  They soon learned that you don't mess with a Rice and his breakfast … the potato pancake was tasty.

3    Betsy continues to facilitate Bible studies through Stonecroft Ministries.  Ben and Betsy have also been blessed to join a Christian "Life Group."  The other group members have become accustomed to unusual prayer requests that include the specific width of a rack spread and number of antlers.

2    Zach moved into an apartment that allows dogs, so he now has another mouth to feed.  Unfortunately, Roo the Chihuahua doesn't appreciate fried venison steaks as much as Zach does.

1    Our biggest reason to be thankful is, of course, the Reason for the Season … our Savior, Jesus Christ.  He has blessed us with family and friends like you, freedom, health, and best of all, eternal life for all who accept His free gift!  While we grieve the loss of Uncle Ted, we also celebrate that he has a head start on heaven!


Here's praying this Christmas season finds you filled with love, joy, good health, and gratitude ~    Ben & Betsy

Sadly Christmas cards and letters are becoming a thing of the past. Even if you don't participate in this seasonal activity, apply the "how to share without bragging" concept to other areas of your life. Friends and family do want to know what's happening with you and your loved ones; don't deny them the opportunity to see beyond the surface. And don't hesitate to use a bit of humor to soften the discomfort of sharing details. Not everyone is comfortable sharing personal information; move out of your comfort zone to become more of a "sharer."

 ACTION

Acquire a taste for something that is out of your comfort zone.

Maybe it's wine, maybe it's opera music ... or maybe it's skydiving.

I don't enjoy opera music, but I recognize the value of it. I appreciate the talent and purity of well-done opera. I never, however, have acquired the kind of appreciation that connoisseurs have. I envy those who get washed away in ecstasy by a good opera.

The same used to be true for me in terms of my limited appreciation for coffee and tea ... and even wine. My parents were 5-cup-a-day coffee drinkers, yet I never touched the stuff. I loved the smell of the freshly brewed java wafting into my bedroom each morning, but the taste was a different story.

It wasn't until the early 90's when I was working at a company that had a coffee pot every 10 yards that I drank my first cup of coffee. Wisconsin had a string of sub-zero days that left my hands nearly numb when I got to the office each morning. In desperation, I poured myself a cup of coffee to use as a hand warmer. I added some cream, just like Mom and Dad used to. I choked down a small swallow, just to see if it would warm my insides. Ick. I choked down another swallow. Less icky.

By my third swallow, I was feeling warmer and didn't hate the taste. The rest, as they say, is history, as I now can't even dream of eating a cookie without a coffee to accompany it.

Think of all the opportunities I missed during my pre-coffee years to have conversations at the coffee pot stations at work. Think of the all the opportunities I missed to relax with my coffee-drinking friends.

I'm still not a habitual morning coffee drinker ... but now I have an appreciation for what a really good cup of java tastes like and how it can enhance a day, a dessert, or a conversation. What can you acquire a taste for, starting today?

## Affinity by Association

Affinities aren't limited to things you've experienced or that you enjoy; they can simply be things that you show an interest in for the purpose of showing you're interested in someone. The interest you show, in itself, is the act of affinity building.

There are some affinity groups I'd love to be in, but I either don't have the talent or the time to do the group justice. For example, many of my friends and relatives are avid sailors. While I have been on a sailboat only once in my life, I can fully appreciate the passion for this sport. I don't envision myself pursuing it, however, so I live it vicariously through others. This certainly doesn't make me a part of the affinity group, but it does give me a "connection" of sorts to the people in it.

## Affinities, Affinities Everywehre!

Affinities are prolific ... everywhere we look we can find things we have in common with other people. Newspaper and magazine articles, daily conversations, novels, TV talk shows, and the internet are filled with examples of people finding these commonalities.

The affinities will start jumping out at you when you read/listen with a bent toward the concept. Here are a couple examples:

Alex, a sales representative from a local window company had an appointment at my home to check out some leaking windows. I do not have a passion for windows or glass. When Alex arrived, I explained to him that I was just getting over a bad cold and cough, so I would keep my distance from him.

"Oh, I'm just getting over a two-week cold myself.....it was the worst. I coughed so hard I could hardly stand it. Three other guys in the office had it, too. I feel for you."

Bing—immediately an affinity. Because Alex shared that he understood what I was going through, I instantly felt at ease with him.

Jeff Deskovic, who was wrongfully convicted of rape and murder, served 16 years in prison, and was cleared and released via DNA evidence in 2006, had this to say about his prison time:

*I served most of my sentence at a maximum security facility in Elmira, NY. The inmates were of every age, background and temperament you can imagine. But sports were a point of commonality. At meals, in the yard, in the cell block, we'd argue about favorite teams and athletes. We'd have the same conversations—Who belongs in the Hall of Fame? Is LeBron better than Kobe?—that our peers on the outside were having in bars and barbershops. Sports talk was also a way to build relationships with the guards. We'd even place bets and run our version of office pools, wagering cigarettes and stamps and items from the commissary. –Sports Illustrated,* February 4, 2013

Their mutual passion for sports broke down—or at least chiseled small holes though—huge barriers among these inmates and guards.

What small holes can you chisel in barriers that exist between you and someone you have yet to build a relationship with? Work at becoming an intentional "chiseler."

## Affinities: Where It Began

It's been around for over 2,000 years.

We mortals didn't invent this affinity thing—God did.

If you read the Bible, you'll come across a bounty of affinity examples. God's Word in the Holy Bible illuminates the concept of affinity ... in fact, His Word is what prompted me to write this book.

> *For we do not have a high priest who is unable to empathize with our weaknesses, but we have one who has been tempted in every way, just as we are* ... Hebrews 4:15 (New International Version of Holy Bible)

The epitome of affinity came when God, in His infinite wisdom, created Jesus as a man to walk on earth among humans. God knew that we could better understand and relate to Him if we could identify with His "humanness." Jesus had the potential for affinity with humans in every way except sin. He felt pain, He ate food, He worked for a living, He had parents and siblings, He was ridiculed, He was ignored, He was worshiped, He suffered, and He died.

God loved us enough to show Himself as a human being with feelings, temptations, and needs. "Jesus wept," the shortest verse in the Bible, is just one example of how the Creator of the Universe can totally relate to what it's like to be a human being liven in a fallen world.

For Christians, the fact that Jesus rose from the dead and joins His Father for eternity in heaven is really the defining affinity. We want to be like, have a passion for, share in the joy of, and participate in, that same eternal union.

Not only did God demonstrate affinity, but He asks us to be in affinity with Him and each other:

> *Rejoice with those who rejoice, weep with those who weep.*

> - ROMANS 12:15 (ENGLISH STANDARD *VERSION*)

> *So if there is any encouragement in Christ, any comfort from love, any participation in the Spirit, any affection and sympathy, complete my joy by being of the same mind, having the same love, being in full accord and of one mind.*

> –PHILIPPIANS 2:1-2 (ESV)

In Acts 17, Paul demonstrated how to break through barriers and establish dialogue. He talked with the Athenians about something of common interest---worshiping God. Similarly, we can use sports talk, current events talk, gardening talk—the possibilities are endless----to break down barriers and strike up a conversation.

But the bottom line of affinity—and, indeed, of relationship building—is that you CARE about people and LOVE them as human beings. Only when care and love are present can real affinity-building begin.

## The 101 of the 101

Let's end this 101 chapter with one of the most basic actions:

 ACTION

| Smile! |
| --- |

This is self-explanatory … or is it? When we smile at someone, we give the message that we acknowledge we're in relationship with them, even if in a very superficial, temporary way. A mutual smile on their part "seals the deal" and creates a mini affinity circle of two people who reached out to each other at one point in time.

My Rotary Club hosted an exchange student from Bulgaria several years ago. When I asked him what was one of the things that surprised him the most about the United States, he said, "Everybody looks at you here and smiles. We don't do that in my country." It turns out that Bulgarians typically don't use smiles to diffuse tension like we do here in the US. Can you imagine walking through life, down streets, down the halls of school, down grocery store aisles, rarely being smiled at? I can't. In most languages and cultures, it's the simple act of a smile that affirms the bond of humanity. Even in cultures like Bulgaria that reserve smiles for "when they have a reason to smile," the curving up of the lips is a way to say, "we're in this human-thing together."

# 3

---

## Building Affinity In The Workplace

*If there is any great success in life, it lies in the ability to put yourself in the other person's place and to see things from his point of view—as well as your own.*

– HENRY FORD

"WHAT IF YOU don't have any affinity with your boss?" asked a colleague when I bounced the idea for this book off of her.

"Then you're not trying hard enough," was my initial reaction. "What are you doing to uncover those affinities? For starters, you both have a passion for this place and the people we serve. I'm sure if you dig more, you'll find that there are a lot more bonds with your boss than you think."

If you feel you don't have any affinity or bond with your co-workers or your boss or your neighbors, it's because you're not trying hard enough to see the connections.

If you're a manager, the onus is on you to initiate the affinity-building process. If you're a team member with a manager who isn't an affinity builder, you may need to take the first steps.

Success is at the intersection of each strong relationship you build.

## Basics in workplace affinity building

Whether you're a CEO or in an entry-level position, it's crucial to understand some basic communication phenomena related to affinities. Because they are basic building blocks of our personality, affinities affect everything from the people we hang out with to how we interpret data to what we eat for dinner.

To illustrate how your past experiences affect your viewpoint, say aloud the first thing that comes to mind when you see: **ERA**

I've asked a variety of people. Their responses included the following:

- Earned Run Average
- Equal Rights Amendment
- the laundry detergent
- a period of time
- a real estate company

It's highly likely that your first response was the direct result of what your brain has the most experience with, or what captures your interest the most. My friends who are avid baseball fans think "earned run average" when they see "ERA." I tend to look at it as a word that indicates a period of time (probably because I love words, and I see ERA as a word and not as an abbreviation). You get the picture.

I was recruited to be a personal banker early in my career. "But," I explained to the bank president who thought I'd be a good fit, "I'm not a numbers person."

"That's OK," he said. "Neither am I." He talked me into it, and I began my training in various areas of the bank, including the teller line. I loved the interaction with the customers and was starting to understand that my affinity for people trumped my lack of enthusiasm for money and finance.

On my third day of training at the teller window, a customer withdrew $10,000 and said he was going to buy some CDs. Wow, I thought to myself (and, thankfully didn't say out loud), that's going to be a truckload of CDs. It wasn't until the customer was seated in front of a personal banker that I realized he meant Certificates of Deposit and not Compact Discs. And, no, I didn't stay in banking very long.

The point of that story? Leading up to that job, I was shaped by the things for which I had an affinity. Clearly, music and pop culture held much more of an affinity to me than finance. It didn't take me long to realize that I could use my communication skills and love for people in a way that better suited my affinities. Banking just wasn't for me.

## Affinity and Employee Retention

*If every member of a team doesn't grow together they will grow apart.*

−SIMON SINEK, BRITISH/AMERICAN AUTHOR AND
SPEAKER

It's not rocket science that employees who are happy, engaged, and satisfied at work are less likely to look for another job. The science part lies in the ways we can measure employee engagement. The Gallup Company is a leader in this area, and its "Gallup Q12 Index" uses thirty years of in-depth behavioral economic research involving more than seventeen million employees to predict employee engagement and workgroup performance. The survey tool asks twelve yes/no questions that are linked to key business outcomes.

One of the questions asked as part of the Q12 survey is "Do you have a best friend at work?" This question may strike you as odd, especially if you've been indoctrinated into a "work is work, and personal life is personal life" mentality.

If you have a best friend at work, it means there is at least one individual there with whom you have established affinities. From a metrics standpoint, employees who report having a best friend at work were:

- 43% more likely to report having received praise or recognition for their work in the last seven days.
- 37% more likely to report that someone at work encourages their development.
- 35% more likely to report coworker commitment to quality.
- 28% more likely to report that in the last six months, someone at work has talked to them about their progress.
- 27% more likely to report that the mission of their company makes them feel their job is important.
- 27% more likely to report that their opinions seem to count at work.
- 21% more likely to report that at work, they have the opportunity to do what they do best every day.

*Business Journal* (May 26, 1999)
I designed a one-hour Affinity-Building Workshop to jump-start a team's affinity-building skills. It's easy to see why I'm passionate about

facilitating these workshops, based on how they can become a small start for culture change. No, I don't profess to help team members become best friends after one hour, but I do give them tools to help foster friendships in and out of the workplace. The same skills carry over into their jobs and can easily be transferred to customer service/sales relationships.

## NCAA Brackets: An unlikely affinity starting point

When I worked in sales for a regulatory compliance company in the 90's, I couldn't name one college basketball player. So why did I participate in the NCAA March Madness playoff bracket competition? Because it was a great way to build affinity. The fact that so many of my co-workers followed the games with enthusiasm drew me to get involved. Today, in fact, I follow college basketball (GO, BADGERS!) fairly closely and ALWAYS fill out a playoff bracket.

My daughter and several of her co-workers at the Fortune 500 company where she worked took a vacation day during March Madness to hang out at a sports bar. The morning—yes, because games start in the AM, one must claim a barstool early—starts with a comparison of brackets and predictions (and perhaps a Bloody Mary). By the end of the day, these co-workers from a variety of departments have a tight bond that transcends their corporate work environment. From IT geeks to C-suite executives to administrative assistants, the camaraderie achieved by this voluntary off-site experience often leads to "friendships" in the workplace.

## Does Your Boss Care About You?

Ponder another one of the 12 questions in the Gallup Employee Engagement Questionnaire:

*Does your supervisor, or someone at work, seem to care about you as a person?*
A "yes' answer to this question—and gosh, I really hope you can answer "yes"—implies that you have some type of affinity with your boss or someone else at work. Sadly, many people I've informally surveyed tell me they don't feel their boss cares about them.

A "no" answer to this question not only implies a lack of affinity-building in a workplace; it also may have serious employee retention implications.

One in two employees has left a job to get away from their manager.

That's *half* of all workers in the US, according to Gallup's report, "State of the American Manager: Analytics and Advice for Leaders," which provides an in-depth look at management, talent, and engagement, based on over four decades of extensive research.

So, what do employees need and want from their managers? In a *Business Journal* article Jim Harter and Amy Adkins present some ideas about the Gallup report. Check out an excerpt.

## Reliable and Meaningful Communication

*Communication is often the basis of any healthy relationship, including the one between an employee and his or her manager. Gallup has found that consistent communication -- whether it occurs in person, over the phone or electronically -- is connected to higher engagement. For example, employees whose managers hold regular meetings with them are almost three times as likely to be engaged as employees whose managers do not hold regular meetings with them.*

*Gallup also found that engagement is highest among employees who have some form (face to face, phone or digital) of daily communication with their managers. Managers who use a combination of face-to-face, phone and electronic communication are the most successful in engaging employees. And when employees attempt to contact their manager, engaged employees report their manager returns their calls or messages within 24 hours. These ongoing transactions explain why engaged workers are more likely to say their manager knows what projects or tasks they are working on.*

*But mere transactions between managers and employees are not enough to maximize engagement. Employees value communication from their manager not just about their roles and responsibilities, but also about what happens in their lives outside of work. The Gallup study revealed that employees who feel as though their manager is invested in them as people are more likely to be engaged.*

*The best managers make a concerted effort to get to know their employees and help them feel comfortable talking about any subject, whether it is work related or not. A productive workplace is one in which people feel safe -- safe enough to experiment, to challenge, to share information and to support one another. In this type of workplace, team members are prepared to give the manager and their organization the benefit of the doubt. But none of this can happen if employees do not feel cared about.*

*Great managers have the talent to motivate employees and build genuine relationships with them. Those who are not well-suited for the job will likely be uncomfortable with this "soft" aspect of management. The best managers understand that each person they manage is different. Each person has different successes and challenges both at and away from work. Knowing their employees as people first, these managers accommodate their employees' uniqueness while managing toward high performance. –* (excerpt from *Employees Want a Lot More From Their Managers* by Jim Harter and Amy Adkins; *Business Journal*; April 8, 2015)

Again, not rocket science. Building *genuine* relationships—and that can't be done without building affinity—is key to motivating and retaining employees.

## Special challenge of family-owned businesses

An owner of a small family-owned business told me "I don't need to build affinities with my employees because they're my children." That flippant but honest remark illustrates a common mistake family-owned businesses make in terms of building external affinities. Family members are so comfortable (or uncomfortable) with the affinities they've built over many years of living together that they often don't see beyond their family ties. True, many family businesses set good boundaries between their family lives and their work lives. However, what these professionals are often missing is the opportunity to build external affinities with each other in the workplace setting.

Family-owned businesses face the unique dilemma of familial affinities vs. company loyalty. In an interview with an officer of a family-owned firm, "Greg" said that it constantly rubbed him the wrong way that his brother got paid the same salary he did, even though his brother did half the work. "But," Greg explained, "he's my brother and I have to have Christmas and Easter dinner with him, and our mom and dad want it this way, so what am I supposed to do?"

Greg continued, "It's kind of like a drug-abuse counselor who is in recovery trying to build a bond with her client—because they're both addicts—and the counselor has to draw the line between "befriending" the client and professionally empowering him. The loyalty is to the professional purpose of counseling, but the urge to befriend someone with similar struggles is very tempting and often distracting. I feel that conflict every day at work. Is my loyalty supposed to be primarily to my brother or to the company?"

The advice I have, regardless of whether you manage a family member or non-family member, is simple—not easy, but simple:

**Build bridges with your employee that transcend your workplace, but honor the professional standards in your workplace.**

## What's in a Name?

 ACTION

When you introduce yourself to someone new, always use both your first and last name.

This sounds counterintuitive, as we feel that being on a "first-name" basis with someone means that we're friends. Set that notion aside on your first meeting, and do each other the favor of exposing more than "Bob" or "Judy." Your first name—and middle name, for that matter—has a story behind it. And your last name indicates what "tribe" you're from. That tribal connection is important and commonly elicits an automatic affinity response: "Oh, did you know Harry Rozelle?" or "I used to work with a Theresa Rozelle—any relation?" ... or, of course, "Any relation to Pete Rozelle?" Yes, by the way, my husband's family is shirt-tail relation to Pete Rozelle, but never close enough to score any free Super Bowl tickets. (And, for those of you with no affinity to the NFL, the late Pete Rozelle was an NFL commissioner).

Take advantage of the built-in affinity opportunity every time you meet someone new. Not only does talking about someone's name build affinity, but it also helps you to remember the name! "Vaya, what a lovely name; is there a story behind it?" or "Is Evans an English name?" etc.

 ACTION

Use "we" more than "I."

*Yesterday, my leadership team met to approve the annual budget.*
*Yesterday, our leadership team met to approve the annual budget.*

One word changes the sentence significantly. Look for opportunities to use "our," "we," and "they" in your daily communications. The inclusive approach reminds everyone that "we're in this together." The overuse of "I" often comes across as egotistical.

There are glaring differences in the way various political leaders use the "I." Some elected officials and those running for office, for instance, use it to the extreme, almost forgetting that they're representing a constituency. Take note during the next election cycle. You'll hear a lot of "I promise to …" instead of "With your help and the team we have assembled, we will …"

## Practice together

The more you work and practice together, the higher your chance of building affinity. Sounds obvious, right? Well, it's true only if you deliberately seek to learn more about each other. And, just like any other skill, affinity-building requires time and practice.

I was part of a group of co-workers that entered a community Pictionary contest. To prepare for working efficiently as a team, we played Pictionary over our lunch hours a few times. Drawing is not my forte, so when I picked the word *amputate* in a practice round, my teammates were not able to figure out the meaning behind my stick figure with an "x" through its leg. And, my knife-wielding stick figure doctor didn't help, either. We guffawed when our time was up, and I tried to justify my perfectly logical and simple drawing.

Two weeks later, halfway into our first round of real competition, it was my turn to draw. Defying all odds, the word on my card was—yes, you guessed it—*amputate*. I didn't try to suppress the funny grin and giggle, and literally before I put pencil to paper, one of my teammates yelled "amputate!" It was embarrassing explaining to the suspicious judges what led to this seemingly telepathic guess.

Time spent together toward a common goal leads to familiarity which leads to affinity, which leads to success.

 ACTION

| Spread the word! |
| --- |

When somebody gives you some advice or a recommendation that is helpful, your first reaction should be to thank the person who gave you the advice. Your second reaction should be to spread the word to someone else who could benefit!

My daughter shared this e-mail she received at work:

> Bree-
> It was a pleasure to meet you at the academy. It was a lot of fun and very informational. Just wish I could have spent more time but was trying to balance a busy office, home life and get the most out of the Academy.
>
> Wanted to give you a HUGE THANK YOU! Not sure if you remember our discussion about my husband and his heart surgery and limitations on his diet but you told me about PB2. I went to the store on my way home Wed and bought a jar. What a hit! My husband loves it and of course with all the fat removed it's on his diet. The other plus is my dad has pancreatitis and can't have fat either so he was excited too. They both instantly said, "it even tastes like peanut butter!" We told the cardiac rehab therapist about it and she is going to share that with her cardiac patients. I love it that you were able to share something that I will forever remember you for. Thanks for the great tip, I will be figuring out other ways to use it. Take care and hope to see you again soon.
>
> Thank you again!
> Deborah ------------

Deborah's sharing of the PB2 suggestion with her husband, father, and husband's therapist will no doubt have ripple effects for years to come.

And, the fact that Deborah reached back to Bree to thank her affirms the affinity and makes their budding professional relationship stronger.

Need I remind you that none of this is rocket science! It's about *being intentional in your attempts to build affinity.*

## People Long to Belong

Best-selling author and marketer, Seth Godin, talks about affinity a lot ... he just uses other words for it. His February 25, 2015 blog *'Connect to' vs. 'Connect,'* lends insight into the difference between building affinity ("connecting") and simply "connecting to."

> *An organization might seek to 'connect to' its customers or constituents. Connection is a form of permission, the ability to deliver value to the people who request it. Vertical connection creates the ability to communicate and delivers a barrier to entry. Most online stores are connected to their customers. Most freelancers seek to connect to their clients. Most teachers work to connect to their students.*
>
> *That's different, though, than 'connect'. When you connect your customers or your audience or your students, you're the matchmaker, building horizontal relationships, person to person. This is what makes a tribe. People caring about people. Side by side, multiplying exponentially.*
>
> *Organizations are afraid of connecting. They are afraid of losing control, of handing over power, of walking into a territory where they don't always get to decide what's going to happen next. When your customers like each other more than they like you, things can become challenging.*
>
> *Of course, connecting is where the real emotions and change and impact happen.*(February 25, 2015 blog by Seth Godin)

Being the "matchmaker" and building horizontal relationships does, indeed, take a deliberate effort. You're reading this book because you want to become a better connector.

The concept of affinity has led marketing strategists to use "connectors," consumers who receive free samples of products and are encouraged to recommend them to family and friends. Why is this approach successful? Because people *want* to build affinity.

Companies who use connectors to help them market products and services are capitalizing on our human nature. We want to be like others, to have things in common, to belong.

This theory implies that in the question of "is it art imitating life or life imitating art?" the answer is almost always "art imitating life." We're attracted to the movie, song, or painting because it's something *to which we can relate*.

Good customer service makes people feel like they belong, like they have an affinity with not only the product or service but with the company or staff from which they purchased it. Case in point: the Saturn automobile. Boy, was I sad the day I found out Saturn was going out of business. Never have I had a more dependable car than my 2004 Saturn Vue (which I named *Vinnie*), and never have I experienced better customer service than when I purchased it. The minute I walked in the door of the Bergstrom Saturn dealership in Appleton, Wisconsin, I felt like part of the proverbial family. The reputation Saturn had built for its cult-like following was well-earned. My salesman, Jason, took me on a tour of the dealership; literally every person we passed smiled and greeted me.

From the way Jason explained the method of construction (by actual Americans in the actual United States) to the way he took genuine pride in working for the dealership, there was an air of inclusiveness … and I wanted to be part of it. That's good customer service; that's affinity building!

By the way, as of 2018, I'm still driving Vinnie.

## Public Speaking

If you're invited to speak to a special interest group (such as a chamber of commerce or an environmental rights group), don't assume that everyone in your audience has the same affinity for your point of view, your topic, or for the obvious "party line" of the special interest group.

When I worked in the non-profit world, I sat through dozens of presentations at poverty conferences, mentoring summits, and human services retreats in which the speakers assumed I and everyone in the audience was a liberal. Anecdotally, most people in non-profit work tend to lean left politically; I was an exception. It irritated me when speakers would bash certain politicians, thinking everyone in the audience felt the same way about issues. Yes, the speakers were building affinity with a majority of the listeners, but some of us were being alienated. A better tactic would be to at least acknowledge that "some of you may feel that the current governor's policy on this issue is … "

And, conservative public speakers are just as guilty. I'm reminded of a chamber of commerce event where the speaker came out bashing a famous liberal, assuming everyone in the audience would applaud. Guess what. Not all business leaders are conservatives. Public speakers often go too far to pander to their audience, which, in today's culture, is almost always a mixed bag. Unless you're speaking to a Chevrolet convention and want to make a Ford-bashing joke, you're probably safer to assume that not everyone in your audience shares your opinions. Tread lightly when painting broad brushstrokes in your presentations.

 ACTION

| Include a unique personal fact on your bio. |
| --- |

When writing a personal bio or introducing yourself at a meeting or speaking engagement, include more than just the predictable information about yourself. Include at least one unique fact that will score high on some of the audience members' affinity scale (or at least pique their interest). For example, my biography includes the fact that I'm addicted to on-line word games. Not only does this build affinity, but it adds dimension to you as a person and speaker.

**Good:** Tom Smith has been in marketing for 15 years. His undergraduate degree is from the University of California-Berkeley, and he has an MBA from the University of Notre Dame. He's married with 2 children and enjoys bowling and traveling.

**Better:** After 15 years in marketing, Tom says what he likes best about it is the chance to see products and services through the end-users' eyes. He got his undergraduate degree in his hometown at the University of California-Berkeley, and his MBA from the University of Notre Dame. Tom and his wife Tracey have a 10-year-old boy who loves football and a 14-year-old daughter who enjoys anything that has to do with the latest fashions. Tom spends as much time as possible on his passions for traveling and golfing. He's still happy to talk about his hole-in-one on the 11th hole at Kapalua, and he and Tracey recently returned from Italy with a new fondness for really good extra-virgin olive oil.

## The Bottom Line

Some of you are reading this book to get ideas about how to become better at your job (which will often equate to making more money). I respect that.

Author and networking expert Keith Ferrazzi reminds us that "people do business with people they know and like. And people like people who focus on their success. That means a sales call is a success if it advances your customers' cause and builds the relationship, not just if it closes a transaction."

It's counterintuitive for a salesperson to not think about the sale as the "end game." The beauty of affinity-building as a sales tool is that the end game of relationship building often has the side benefit of a sale.

Yes, the bottom line to your boss and board of directors is to make money by selling or producing. But successful producers (sellers, accountants, doctors, etc.) are the ones who focus on the client's best interest. Again, this isn't rocket science; it's a mind shift.

Ferrazzi talks about "generosity without expectations of tit for tat." One of the things he advises is to be prepared with five packets of generosity and no expectation. In other words, go into your meeting with a prospect armed with five ways to make that prospect successful. That's the weapon in Ferrazzi's affinity-building arsenal for gaining people's attention and making them willing to develop a closer relationship with you. Your job is to do the homework it takes to build that arsenal.

*What kind of homework? I'm not talking about the usual research on the company and its need for what you're selling. Research the person! You're looking for personal reasons to care. Find a way to introduce something that leverages your shared interests. Failing that, fall back to some deeply-held personal interests of your own. Talking about them will make you human, not just a sales person pushing a service or a widget.*

*The direct result of focusing so intently on generosity, or even of a single email ping to renew a relationship, is to advance the relationship. But think of it as good sales karma for which you may be rewarded.*

*Recently, as part of coaching a sales team at a major consulting firm, I gave them several relationship-building missions beginning with a generous remembrance on email. The results were telling. Your mileage may vary, but in this case:*

- *One CIO called back immediately, and a week later initiated a dialog about the consulting firm's services.*
- *A senior VP of a global 500 food manufacturer returned the personal message and followed within a week with a request for proposal on Value Chain Transformation.*

- *Another partner was rewarded by being invited to keynote at a conference for a major retailer's top executives.*
- *One managing partner credited the outreach with producing a 750k deal.*

*Imagine the power of offering five packets of generosity. Mind you, they're not all personal. At least one should be purely professional, even if not related in any way to what you're trying to sell. For example, find out what the analysts say the company's goals or "big bets" are and what they have to achieve, and find a way to help the individual serve that cause. Maybe they're breaking into eTail, and you can introduce a well-known eTail guru.*

*I've always said that one or two of your generous offerings can and should be transactional in nature. "I'm going to send you our really informative new collateral to help sell our solution internally."* (Keith Ferrazi's *How to Turn a Relationship Into a Sale; Harvard Business Review,* July 11, 2012)

## Ice Breakers

 ACTION

> When breaking the ice with a new group, ask an open-ended question about the past.

Facilitating groups is one of my passions. Not only do I get to meet new people, but I get to learn about these people. A great way to learn is to ask questions, right? The "ice breaking" stage is the perfect time for asking a question that will reveal something more than skin deep.

When you're responsible for coming up with a way to break the ice with a group, ask a question that'll give you a glimpse into people's childhood. The ordinary ice breaker questions of "why did you join this group?" or "what do you hope to learn today?" or "what is your favorite color?" don't cause people to reveal anything meaningful about themselves. Instead, open-ended questions like, "tell us about your most vivid memory of your first-grade classroom" cause people to tell a short story with their answer.

Ice breaker #1: Please introduce yourself and tell us what your favorite color is.

*My name is Jonathan, and my favorite color is blue.*

Pretty flat and boring, right?

Ice breaker #2: Please introduce yourself (first and last name), and tell us about the first time you ever left the state you were born in.

*My name is Jonathan Knekolic, and I remember my first trip out of Michigan really well. I'm a Yooper (which is what they call those of us from the Upper Peninsula of Michigan), and my family hardly ever went farther than an hour away from home. When I was in 6th grade, we went on a family trip to Disney World in Florida. My dad drew imaginary lines on the back seat so that my little sister and brother and I wouldn't fight. I know we didn't wear any seatbelts, either. The back of the wagon—we had an old Ford station wagon—was stuffed with all of our luggage and a ton of food because my parents were too cheap to stop at restaurants. I remember how cool it was to see the "Welcome" signs for each new state as we headed to Florida. Oh, my folks did break down halfway there and stopped for lunch at a Big Boy.*

There are probably several heads nodding during parts of Jonathan's story, as group members reflect back on their family road trips. An instant bond has taken place.

Some facilitators hesitate to ask open-ended ice breaker questions because they fear it will take up too much time. I feel the time is worth the affinities that are built by allowing group members to reveal some personal information about themselves.

Other ideas for icebreaking/affinity-building questions include:

- Tell us about where you were on September 11, 2001, and how you learned about the attacks.
- When you were a teenager, what did you want to be when you grew up?
- Tell us about the first thing you remember saving your own money to purchase.
- Tell us about the first time you ever left the state you were born in.
- Tell us what you know about how your first and middle names were chosen.

The beauty of these types of questions is that we learn so much more about someone than just the obvious answer. For example, when I ask about where people were on September 11, I invariably hear about how old they were at the time, what type of job (or schooling) they were involved in, and their personal reaction to the tragedy.

When I asked a planning group to introduce themselves with their name, organization, and their most vivid memory from their kindergarten classroom, there was an instant bond when stories were told about mean nuns, chocolate goiter pills, and face-reddening bathroom accidents.

In a corporate visioning session I asked participants to tell about the first thing they remember saving their own money to purchase. One man, so excited about his memory, pulled up a picture on the internet to show us the SS-T Race Car he bought with his allowance as a boy. I immediately flashed back to a Christmas when my cousin Tom got a similar race car and pulled the zip string too close to his sister's hair ... yes, some screaming and crying ensued (and a little muffled laughter). The rest of the room buzzed with similar memories. The point is, we can all relate to childhood toys, and reminiscing together sets a great stage for working together.

Ice "breaking" is a fast process ... but ice "melting'—which is the essence of affinity-building—is a slower process. Finding out someone's favorite color is nice, but what does it really tell you about them? And does it build any type of commonality? It's not a cause for celebration or further conversation to learn that another person in the room also likes the color purple.

And some more actions to help you build affinity in your workplace and community:

 ACTION

Promote a "Word of the Week" in your home or workplace.

When I was the executive director of a non-profit agency, I implemented a silly "Word of the Week" exercise for our staff. I would find a relatively uncommon word—often one I had never heard of—and post it on the meeting board with its definition. Everyone was to use the word in a sentence at least once a day for that week. Needless to say, our staff meetings were often enhanced with some creative uses of that week's featured word. When was the last time, for example, you heard the word *argute* at your office?

 ACTION

Send cards to people who have helped you or who need your help.

Remind them how much you value your affinity with them. I prefer to send and receive hand-written cards ... you know, the ones that actually require getting out a pen and licking an envelope.

 ACTION

When introducing one person to another, mention one thing they may have in common.

"Bob Smith, this is Tammy Jones; Tammy used to be in banking, too." Usually, that's all it takes to get the ball rolling for the new acquaintances.

 ACTION

Be a good audience member.

Make eye contact with the speaker, and show affirmation by nodding at points you can relate to, smiling/laughing when appropriate, and simply showing that you appreciate what s/he is saying. If you aren't in the regular habit of doing this, try it the next time you're in an audience. If the audience is fewer than fifty people, I can almost guarantee that your attentiveness will cause the speaker to increase the number of times s/he looks at you and "connects" with you. It's subtle but important. It's an instant affinity builder, a non-verbal way of saying, "I appreciate what you're saying, and I can relate." Next time you're the speaker, you'll notice the audience members who are expressing affinity with you ... actually, you've always noticed it, but now you'll have an increased awareness of it!

 ACTION

Follow up promptly after meeting someone new.

When you exchange business cards (paper or electronic), follow up with that new contact within 5 business days. Shoot a brief note (handwritten is optimal!) referencing the event/situation that brought you together and at least one thing that brought them to mind that week.

For example, "Hi Bob, it was great meeting you at the American Cancer Society fundraiser on Tuesday. I saw this article today on greyhound rescue dogs and was reminded of you. I hope all is going well with your new dog!"

# 4

---

## Creating Everyday Connections: Building Affinity With Your Family/Neighbors/ Team Members/Faith Community

*Too few people understand a really good sandwich.*

*–JAMES BEARD, AMERICAN COOK AND AUTHOR*

## Six degrees of separation

UNLESS YOU'VE BEEN tortured by the never-ending "It's a Small World" serenade at Disney's Magic Kingdom, you probably have fond associations with the trite "it's a small world" phrase. The Kevin Bacon game of "six degrees of separation" from the 80's underscored the reality of how connected we really are as a human race. This "connectedness" can be the basis for affinity building with anyone you meet. It's always kind of interesting—and sometimes entertaining—to discover the people we have in common. When you meet someone new, be sure to ask them enough questions to help determine if you have an acquaintance in common.

As an adoptee, I've experienced an inordinate amount of the "small world" phenomenon. My birthparents were from Green Bay, WI (only 25 miles north of where I grew up), so the chances of finding the six degrees of separation with my biological family were pretty high. While I never experienced the drama of dating what turned out to be a cousin, I did end up learning—after meeting my birthparents as an adult—my adoptive family had some friends in common with my biological family. This isn't all that odd considering the geographical distance.

Prior to meeting my birthparents I was a big believer in nurture over nature. I now see the two as working closely together to build on the wiring God designed in us. There are times—even though I haven't seen her or spoken to her for many years—that I say or do something and feel like I'm imitating my birthmother. Maybe it's because I lived with her for the first two years of my life; but more likely it's genetic. God gives us a built-in affinity with biological relatives. We can't explain it, but we feel it.

It was when I met my biological father for the first time that I learned of many more connections. Blindsided and thrilled by the thought of my birthfather actually requesting to meet me, my heart raced in anticipation of his arrival. When I met my birthmother a couple weeks earlier, I felt a bond but didn't really see a whole lot of physical similarities.

Then I opened my front door to my biological father, Tom. Big. Brown. Eyes. Like mine.

It was the first time in my life that I actually saw and felt a biological resemblance. It was obvious where my big brown eyes came from; it was equally obvious that my Type A personality was genetic.

Tom brought a photo album with him to help tell his family's story. As I paged through the pictures, I noticed a postcard he had saved from his parents. The address was in Naples, Florida.

"Wow, what a coincidence," I said. "My sister lives in Naples." Keep in mind that we grew up in a small town in Wisconsin, so it was unusual for my 20-something sister to have moved to Naples, a retirement city.

"Yeah, my mom and dad live down there in the winter months," Tom explained.

Then I saw the street address on the postcard: Boca Ciega Drive.

"No way!" I exclaimed. "My sister lives on Boca Ciega Drive." It turns out my sister and grandparents lived in the same apartment complex, shared the same swimming pool, and probably had already crossed paths. My sister (not biological) got to meet them before I did, and we all became part of this neat, albeit uncomfortable, bonding process. Way fewer than six degrees of separation.

 ACTION

> Recognize and embrace the positive similarities you have with your parents.

Take note today of something you do or say that looks, sounds, or feels like something your mother, father, or sibling does or says. Even if you're not biologically related, chances are you still have those "I'm starting to act just like my mom/dad" moments. These revelations of affinity may make you smile or may make you cringe; either way, they're reminders of your unique bond with your parents. Embrace this "affinity" behavior—unless it's chewing with your mouth open like your dad did.

## Support Groups

*What makes loneliness an anguish is not that I have no one to share my burden, but this: I have only my own burden to bear.*

–DAG HAMMARSKJÖLD, SWEDISH DIPLOMAT AND AUTHOR

I worked on this book for more than five years. I kept asking, "Why is this taking so long, and why am I not motivated to finish this thing?" Was I lazy? No. Was I uninspired? No. Was I afraid my words wouldn't be good enough or helpful to anyone? Maybe.

In October 2016 my stepson Zach died from an accidental heroin/ fentanyl overdose. Our family's world was shaken in a way we could never imagine. Only a short time into our grief, we realized that we were called to comfort others in their grief as well. We are now in the "parents who have lost a child through addiction" affinity group. Maybe the purpose of this book's delay was for me to reflect on the importance of ALL of life's experiences, even those that are so painful they're hard to put into words. The deeper the pain, the deeper the affinity with others who have experienced similar pain.

Support groups are the epitome of exploring and utilizing affinities. The internet makes it easier than ever to connect people who are in similar circumstances. The sad reality is that most support groups are formed because of an unfortunate circumstance that members have in common (thus the need for "support"). A beautiful thing about being part of a support group is not that you have suffered the same difficult experience, but that you can share the pain, challenges, comfort, and healing that come from having an affinity with those who have had a similar experience. On Zach's on-line obituary page, thoughts and prayers poured in, many from strangers who simply wanted to reach out to let us know their family experienced loss through addiction as well. What a comfort it was to be comforted by those who understood like no one else can.

As I write this, I'm thinking of the funeral we'll be attending this weekend of another young man in our community who overdosed on heroin. We didn't know him. But now we have a strong understanding of what his parents are experiencing; we want to wrap our arms around them in comfort and hope. That's affinity.

When we find ourselves in these "unfortunate" affinity groups, there are so many different ways to react. For me, sharing the experience with others is my automatic response. Whether the "support group" is formal or informal, there's a solace in sharing, hurting, dealing, and healing together. This post from a Facebook friend whose son has Juvenile Diabetes sums it up:

> *There's an instant connection when you meet someone and their child has the same disease as your own child. You instantly bond. It's a beautiful, sad club to belong to.*

> - LISA CRUZ

It's surprising, then, that many people reject or don't seek out support groups. The reasons vary, but common ones I've seen/heard are:

1. I already have a supportive group of family and friends.
2. I'm embarrassed by the disease (or whatever the unfortunate experience is).
3. If I join a group, it's like admitting I have a problem.
4. I don't want to be defined by this problem.
5. I'm strong enough to handle my own problems.

 ACTION

---

Join a support group.

---

This isn't for everyone or in every season of life, but there will come a time when you are faced with an issue that seems overwhelming or heartbreaking.

If you're struggling with a difficult situation (disease in the family, recovering from victimization of any kind, or any experience that has a lingering negative impact in your life), I strongly encourage you to reach out to others who are "in the same boat." Does that mean you have to pour out your feelings to complete strangers? No, not if you're not comfortable doing that. What it does mean is that you'll learn more about how others cope with the issue, find comfort in being able to comfort others (and be comforted by them), and feel a sense of "belonging" that reminds you you're not alone in the feelings you have.

## Affinities in books and the theater … and everyday life

 ACTION

> Experience things live and in real time!

Whenever possible, go to live musical, theatre, and speaking events. There's increased affinity by being elbow-to-elbow with people of like interests; but you also feel much more attached to the people on stage.

When VCRs became popular, I said, "My bet is that in 10 years, movie theaters will become obsolete. Why go to the theater for $5 (or $7 or $10) when you can rent a movie for less than half the price?" Good thing I didn't bet my life savings on that.

Why are movie theaters still relatively successful even after the advent of DVDs, Amazon Prime, and Netflix? Part of it is because people are impatient and want to see a movie as soon as possible. But I believe a bigger part of it is affinity. People want to *experience* a movie *with other people*—and apparently, the more people the better.

Not only do the people in the theater build affinity by experiencing movies together, but the very movies they're watching are filled with—you guessed it—people building affinity.

And, obviously, live performances trump on-screen and electronic versions. It's not a stretch to say that you're more connected with an actor, speaker, or musician who is literally just feet away from you, than you are with their image on a screen or their voice over your stereo. When George W. Bush was president, I perceived him to be very arrogant and flippant. My view of him changed when I saw him live and up close. The arrogance that showed on television was missing from his "in the flesh" gentle candor.

As an "affinity junkie," I started collecting examples of affinity several years ago. Like a photographer looking for a good shot, my affinity radar is always up. Here are just a handful of the instances I've collected:

> In Jodi Picoult's book *Change of Heart*, Lucius, a gay prison inmate with AIDS says of fellow inmate Calloway, "He was a racist bigot but Calloway was also the best chess player I'd ever met." (p. 55; Washington Square Press)

Their mutual passion for chess broke down (or at least chiseled small holes through) huge barriers between these two inmates.

In the following movie reviews (taken from United Hemispheres magazine, Feb. 2009), notice how the bonds between and among characters—the affinities—are an integral part of the plot:

> *The Family That Preys: Charlotte Cartwright, an affluent socialite, and Alice Pratt, a working class woman, have remained dear friends for many years despite their apparent differences. But they both are ashamed of their children's scandalous behavior ... (pg. 67)*
>
> *Nights in Rodanthe: Adrienne Willis agrees to tend to her friend's inn on the Outer Banks of North Carolina for a weekend. There she meets Dr. Paul Flanner. As a storm rolls in, Adrienne and Paul bond over their current crisis ... (pg. 69)*
>
> Trauma *by Michael Palmer and Daniel Palmer (2015): Dr. Nugent, a married father of two, was a competitive tri-athlete who had finished well ahead of Carrie in the last race they'd done together. Over the years, Carrie had learned that it paid to be friends with the radiologists*

*for situations just like this. And nothing fostered camaraderie quite like the race circuit.*

And, finally, a beautiful illustration of affinity that I found in the tenth chapter of Emily Giffin's novel *First Comes Love:*

*"I don't think I've ever seen you in anything pink," I say, fondly remembering the day I met Ellen, shortly after I moved back to Atlanta from New York. I was behind her in a long line at the post office, sizing up her outfit the way women do with one another, noticing the details of her faded blue jeans, ripped at the left knee and rolled at the ankles, her bold gladiator sandals, olive-green linen tunic, and layers of funky bead-and-leather necklaces. She looked cool in an effortless way, and although she wouldn't have stood out in New York, she made an impression in the Buckhead sea of brightly colored Tory Burch, Lilly Pulitzer, and Lululemon. Then I glanced down at her package and saw the familiar address of my old New York apartment building in black Sharpie: 22C, exactly three floors down from my 25C.*

*"It wasn't like me to chat up strangers, but this coincidence was too great. I tapped her shoulder and said, "I don't mean to be nosy, but your package... That's my old building! I lived in 25C."*

*Her face lit up, instantly elevating her from plain to pretty. "You're kidding! My good friends Hillary and Julian live there. Did you know them?" "No," I said, smiling back at her. "But small world, huh?" She nodded and said, "So you're a New Yorker?" I told her no, I was actually a native Atlantan, but that I'd lived in the city for years. "I miss it," I added. She nodded and said, "I do, too. I lived there for years myself. Why'd you come back? For a job?" "My husband's job," I said. We had only just married, and saying the words my husband still felt so foreign to me. "Same here," she said, then introduced herself as Ellen Graham. I told her my name, and we continued to talk in line. I learned that she was a professional portrait photographer, originally from Pittsburgh, married to a lawyer, and I told her my bare-bones ...*

*She waited as I completed my transaction. Then, on our way out to the parking lot, she reached into her tote bag, handed me a little square business card, and suggested that we go for coffee sometime, maybe grab dinner with our husbands. "I'd love that," I said, feeling that rush of new-friend excitement that becomes rarer the older you get. A few weeks later, I called Ellen, and the four of us went to Leon's Full Service, a restaurant in Decatur . . ."*

The two women went on to become dear friends ... and all because one woman went out of her comfort zone to "chat up a stranger."

 ACTION

Look for examples of affinity building in books, movies, and everyday interactions.

Then, ask yourself what intentional steps were taken to build an affinity. The more attentive you are, the easier it will be for you to become a natural affinity builder.

## Basic affinities

Playing: It's common to see kids at a playground playing with other kids they've never met. Their affinity for play breaks down age, gender, race, and ability barriers.

Many of us have sadly outgrown the ability to let a strong affinity transcend other barriers. Golfers, when was the last time you showed up alone at a golf course and asked to be matched with the next few people who wanted to play 18 holes? If you did, you truly have an affinity for golf that overcomes any awkwardness there may be about playing the game with strangers. Golf, like other activities, is a great affinity builder.

My husband and I used to go to courses with no tee time and offer to be matched with other twosomes. We met some great people this way and also tended to raise our level of play (which isn't saying much) to meet the skill of the other half of our foursome.

 ACTION

> Play interactive games that require conversation and creative communication. You'll be amazed and amused by the things you learn about others.

Golfing may not be your thing, but there are countless other forms of game and sport that will help you build affinity. Interactive games that require creative thinking—such as charades, Balderdash, and Apples to Apples—are excellent affinity-builders. One of my favorite such games is "Heads Up!," a game made popular by Ellen DeGeneres. It's an inexpensive app that provides hours of silly fun. The goal is to get your teammates to guess the word on the card (or on your electronic device) without saying any part of the word or without rhyming. Don't underestimate how much you can learn about people from the way they play these games. I never knew, for example, that my husband could do a spot-on imitation of Bob Dylan, until he and his Heads Up partner outscored my team because of his ability to mimic people. When you're finished laughing at each other after every round, you begin some fun side conversations about the words and phrases from the game.

Food: a universal affinity. Look no further than social media to see the popularity of anything edible. If you can't think of something to talk about, there's always the topic of food. A new recipe, a great restaurant, a horrible dining experience ... any of these will resonate with just about everyone. One of my most popular food-related Facebook posts was an announcement that I was making "Rick's Old Girlfriend's Hot Dish," a recipe from our friends Rick and Mary (and, no, Mary's not the "old girlfriend").

Some of my fondest vacation memories revolve around food. If you've ever had the juice of a food-truck porchetta sandwich drip down your chin while you marveled at the beauty of a Tuscan sunset, you want to talk about that memory. And if you find someone who has savored a really good porchetta sandwich (or any good meal in Tuscany—and dare I say there really isn't a bad meal to be had there), you want to relive that memory by talking about it with someone who can relate. The same is true of any kind of food experience because taste is a larger-than-life sensation that makes eating one of my absolute favorite things to do. And, from what I see on social media and in the world around me, the act of eating seems to be a favorite pastime for a lot of other people, too.

There's something about food that resonates like nothing else. As cook and author James Beard said, 'Food is our common ground, a universal experience." As such, your journey of affinity-building can start with something as simple as talking about the memories you associate with certain foods. In Wisconsin, all you have to do is mention "cheese curds" to get people talking about the squeakiness and utter deliciousness of those luscious pieces of curdled milk. You'll hear stories about where to get the best fresh curds and which restaurant has the best deep-fried curds. Ah, yes, Wisconsinites have an affinity for cheese, in all forms.

## Talk to Strangers

Forget the warning you learned when you were a kid. The "don't talk to strangers" message is good for a five-year-old, but as an adult, don't let it ruin your chances of building affinity. In fact, make it a point to talk to strangers. It could be life changing.

> *My mother and I were having coffee in an outdoor café in Brighton, England, after touring the indescribably opulent*

*Royal Pavilion. I was in my forties then, and I had just explained to my mother how different my reaction to the beauty of the palace was compared to what it would have been when I was in my twenties. A woman at the table next to us said, "Pardon me for eavesdropping, but I overheard what you just said, and I liked how you said it so well that I've written it down. Do you mind if I repeat it to you so that I can see if I got it right?" What an encouragement her words were for the writer in me! ... It turned out that Caroline, the woman who spoke to me, was also in her late forties and understood exactly what I meant. For the next half-hour, we discussed how our priorities and our focus change as we grow older. Caroline's request that I repeat my words was a turning point in my confidence to pursue writing as a vocation."*

-THE CREATIVE CALL (JANICE ELSHEIMER), P. 58

My husband is particularly skilled—sometimes exasperatingly so—at talking to people he has just met. Often I have to pull him away from a conversation he has struck up with strangers. But just as often, I get pulled into that conversation ... and I'm always glad.

 ACTION

---

Talk to strangers.

---

It's fine if the conversation is about the weather at first, but look for cues that may lead to an affinity. Take advantage of long lines (or queues, as the British call them). You have an obvious affinity with the people you're standing in line with ... you're all going to the same movie, you all have groceries to be scanned, you're all waiting for the blockbuster Christmas specials, etc. Use your waiting time to build on your commonality.

Even if you're simply striking up a conversation about the weather, use add-ons that act as openers for affinity building.

"Wow, it's a beautiful day," is friendly, but a dead end.

"Wow, what a beautiful day to take a bike ride. Have you ever tried the new trails they just opened outside of town?" is an affinity opener. The worst that could happen is the person could respond with, "No, I'm not into biking," to which you could reply, "So, what's your ideal way to spend a day like this?"

Back when scrapbooking was popular, I was about the 50th person in line at a Club Scrap warehouse sale. I let everyone around me know I was a "Club Scrap virgin." They showered me with advice and tips on how to navigate the sale. We bonded because I was a fellow scrapper, and the ladies were happy to share their expertise with me. Before long, we were talking about how we spend the holidays and where we worked.

Don't miss the opportunity to practice your affinity-building skills with these actions:

 ACTION

| Go to weddings and funerals. |
| --- |

Go to every wedding to which you're invited ... and don't skip the ceremony.

You'll catch up with friends and family you don't see often, and you'll meet new people who are somehow connected to the happy couple. Oh, and there's cake ...

Make funerals of loved ones and friends a priority. Don't go just to the visitation; stay for the service and any reception that follows. There's nothing better than strengthening relationships while enjoying ham sandwiches and green Jello (in Wisconsin, there may be marshmallows or grated carrots in it). The funeral is the time for everyone to share stories about their memories of the deceased. You are automatically bonded because of your mutual loss.

 ACTION

> Wear logo apparel.

Don't hesitate to wear clothing that features logos of your company, your alma mater, or your favorite team or group. Comment on other people's logo apparel.

My husband and I were in an archive library on the Island of Jersey (off the northern coast of France) searching for clues about his French heritage. We had not yet come upon any other Americans on the island, and it seemed like we were the only people who didn't quite have the "drive on the left side of the road" thing down very well.

"Are you from Appleton?" an American-sounding voice behind me asked.

Realizing she had read the address on the back of the "Rozelle Construction, Appleton WI" tee shirt I was sporting, I eagerly turned and responded "That's where he (pointing at my husband, Ben) grew up and has his construction business."

"Wow, what a coincidence. My brother lives there," said my fellow American. "We're from Ohio, but we come to Wisconsin a lot."

Needless to say, our conversation led us into many affinities, including the fact that we were all there to search for family heritage.

Had I not worn that tee shirt that day, I'm certain that fortuitous conversation wouldn't have happened.

This Facebook post from Ben's cousin, Paul—accompanied by a picture of a Green Bay Packers headband—is another great example of how your clothing can build affinity:

*Good start to a very cold Boston morning. Walking downtown wearing this when a very large man crosses the street yelling something at me. It is a challenge to know if such situations should be addressed with a defensive big city posture or Midwestern hospitality. Curious, I slowed down at his approach. It was then that everything became clear. He lifted his work cap and scarf to reveal his own Packer hat, pointed to the G, and shouted again, "Hey my man, we are running the table baby!" We high fived and moved on. An unusual but welcome experience in Patriots country.*

## Reading the same words

When I read a good book, I can't wait to recommend it to others. Obviously, I want others to enjoy what I've enjoyed, but I also want to develop another affinity with other readers. When we read the same materials as someone else, we develop a new bond with them that we didn't have before. It's a simple concept, but an important one, as it relates to this affinity model I'm trying to develop.

I have a confession to make: I've become an "electronic" reader. Those who know me may be surprised to learn that I've largely abandoned paperback and hardcover book reading. I download e-books and audio books free, using my library card. And, yes, I read/listen to those books on my smartphone. Ugh, I never thought it would happen to me, but I *like* it.

Why do I feel the need to confess this sin against 'real' books? Because the act of holding a physical book in your hand in a public setting is a great way to build affinity, and I'm denying myself that opportunity. When you walk past someone in a coffee shop, on a train, or in a library, and they are holding a book, it's an automatic conversation-starter. What a person is reading speaks volumes about them and is an opening to a conversation. "Oh, I just finished that book! Isn't it fantastic? He's one of my favorite authors." You can't see the book cover when someone is reading on a Kindle. You get the idea.

Our embrace of the electronic culture, while it has created new and interesting ways to interact with people, is also robbing us of some dear connections. Think of how cell phones, for example, have changed the way we interact. Thirty years ago, if your mom called to talk to you at college, one of your roommates may have answered the phone. Mom would have asked him how he and his parents were doing, and then he would have put you on the phone. When you call your college son today, not only do you not stand a chance of talking to his roommates, you probably get your boy's voice mail. He'll text you back. Ah, the double-edged sword of technology. But that's for another book ...

Affinity comes from experiencing similar things. True, we don't all experience things the same way, but we often experience the same things. So it is with the books we read and the TV shows we watch.

My local library has joined the thousands across the country that sponsor Community Book Reads. The community is encouraged to read the same book and come together to discuss it. There's value in that. It's neat to hear other viewpoints on the same words, and it's gratifying to be affirmed about our viewpoints. Most important, though, is that the Community Book Read gives people an excuse to get together.

 ACTION

Participate in your local Community Book Read.

If your local library doesn't have such a thing, start one! Create a new affinity today by inviting someone (a stranger even!) to read the same book you're reading.

 ACTION

---

**Use figures of speech.**

---

Unless you're writing the great American novel or an objective news story, it's OK to frequently use figures of speech. This is contrary to what your creative writing teacher may have told you, but this isn't about writing. It's about relationship building. Go out on a limb, take the bull by the horns, and relish the small world we live in.

 ACTION

---

**Make it a habit to pay genuine compliments to people every day.**

---

Why? It shows you have an affinity (e.g. an appreciation) for something they've done or said ... not to mention the benefit of making someone's day brighter with your kind words.

 ACTION

---

Go to as many garage sales (rummage sales, tag sales, estate sales) as you can.

---

You don't even need to buy anything to build affinity.

What can be more "personal" than someone inviting you onto their yard or into their garage to peruse their clothes, dishes, and furniture? Take advantage of these bonding experiences by starting conversations with fellow rummagers and the hosts. The thrill of a bargain is a unique affinity. Ask about the background of an item you buy: "So, did you catch any big fish with this pole?" Every item at a garage sale has a story, and each story is connected to a person.

## Unlikely Affinities

I met Stanley, a retired art teacher, and his wife Pamela in Maui. Stanley invited us to see their Kahana Sunset condo that was decorated with his beautiful artwork (an affinity for my husband Ben).

Pamela "confessed" that she's a smoker. Since smoking on lanais there is against the rules, she goes out to the parking lot. She meets other smokers whose only obvious affinity is nicotine. This "negative" affinity has been the foundation of many relationships, between and among smokers who now find themselves in the sometimes-ostracized minority. It's not uncommon to see a businessman in a suit and tie standing outside a smoke-free building puffing away next to a custodian in overalls. Their habit brought them together.

Ben and I, along with his cousin, rode to the Kahalui, Maui airport together on "Executive Shuttle" service. Two other couples joined us, and they appeared to be much more affluent and "proper" than we (although that wouldn't take much). As the shuttle service's name indicated, it typically catered to people who fit the stereotype of "executive."

Conversation on the shuttle turned to the tightening of airline regulations and the changing roles of flight attendants. That led to a conversation about pilots.

Ben said, "Did you guys ever see that episode with the pilots on *The Man Show*?"

Our driver grinned and said, "I was just thinking of that same exact show!"

Ben and the driver rehashed the episode bit by bit as they re-enacted the men dressed as pilots and sitting in an airport bar getting drunk two hours before they were to fly a commercial airplane.

Our shuttle was soon filled with guffawing and exchanges among four of the men, "Did you see the episode where … "

The driver joked, "I don't usually get such high-brow customers." We built on our low-brow affinities for the remainder of the hour-long trip. No wonder people assume all Wisconsinites own cheesehead hats.

Speaking of wearing cheese on one's head, my in-laws are avid Packers fans—the hang-the-Packers-flag-outside-on-every-game-day type of people. Interestingly, though, if the Packers don't make the playoffs, their allegiance turns to whichever teams made it from our division. The very teams that were our archenemies during the season (can you say Minnesota Vikings?) all of a sudden become the teams to cheer for. Personally, I draw the line at supporting the Vikings, but you get the idea.

My husband Ben is not the stereotypical "biker" type. He doesn't wear leather, he doesn't have a tattoo, and he's never been to a rally. But when he cruises down the road on his Harley Davidson, he becomes "one of them." It took him a while to notice, but whenever he'd encounter fellow bikers on the road, they'd flash a horizontal peace sign to him ... a symbol of affinity, basically saying, "Greetings, dude, you're one of us."

Sometimes our affinity is one step away from the person standing in front of us. It may be a connection through our parents instead. For example, I buy a poppy every year from the service veterans who sell them in front of grocery stores during Veteran's Day week. I immediately feel not only a huge sense of gratitude to these men and women, but also an affinity for them and for their families because my dad was a veteran also.

Bottom line: treat people who aren't in your affinity circle as if they soon will be. It's up to YOU to discover those intersections and then build upon them.

 ACTION

When you host a party, give it a title.

Cheryl Najafi, author of the book *You're So Invited: Panic Less, Play More, and Get Your Party On!*, says that "when you title an event—say a Funny Hat Party or a Chili Cook-Off—you instantly give it a personality. Everyone will feel comfortable and on the same plane."

I tired of hosting parties that involved selling things. You know the stuff I'm talking about: kitchenware, candles, makeup, etc. The only reason I would have these get-togethers is to have an excuse to get some friends together for fun and snacks. I hated the idea of them feeling obligated to purchase something (read, the $37 pizza stone they would never use). So twelve years ago I began hosting an annual party that involved NOT BUYING THINGS! It's called WEB (Women Exchanging Belongings). Friends bring books, jewelry, accessories, décor, and housewares they don't want anymore and exchange them for "new" items from friends ... all while indulging in chitchat, giggling, wine, and appetizers. It's fun to hear the background of the items that are brought: "I bought this scarf on a whim from an art fair, and I never wore it," or "my sister gave me this for Christmas and it doesn't match with anything; don't tell her I'm giving it away."

 ACTION

> Go to every class reunion.

I realize some of you feel it's best to "leave the past behind." I get that, to a certain extent. On the other hand, no one knows you in the same way your high school friends do. True, you may be a totally different person now, but your teenage memories are forever linked with your high-school classmates. Who else in my life experienced the "wrath of Esch" if you yawned during his class ... or can remember the fruited Jello that ALWAYS accompanied the too-small pizza burgers at lunch? Only my high-school classmates. It's worth going to the reunions just to reminisce about those silly affinities that are unique to your circle of high-school friends.

# 5

## Meet Me On-Line: Electronic/Social Networking

*In Social Media the "squeaky wheel" gets the oil. You have to put yourself out there, to find people who will relate or even debate with you, depending on what you are looking for.*

— Jessica Northey, Social Media Entrepreneur

NEVER IN OUR history has it been easier to reach out to vast numbers of people. Social media is "affinity in motion." If you're going to be intentional about building affinity and connecting with people, you must be intentional about how you use social media. As Northey says, you have to put yourself out there.

My daughter accuses me of "liking" too many things on Facebook. Guilty as charged. I click my reaction to Facebook posts often to let people know I relate to what they're saying. That's important to me. And I hope it's important to you.

 ACTION

> Use social media to its fullest.

Use all forms of social media to connect friends and strangers to yourself and each other. Use Instagram, Twitter, Facebook, and other social media as the affinity tools they're designed to be. Be intentional. Be specific. Be generous with your responses to others.

Note the difference between two Facebook posts about the same business conference:

Felicia's post: *I'm at a work conference instead of being outside.*

Jordan's post: *Just had the best fettuccine alfredo of my life at the "Improving Your Sales Skills Conference." Blown away by tonight's keynote speaker's message about prospecting tools. (Link to speaker's web page).*

Which post do you think generated the most interest and connections? Would you rather attend the conference with Felicia or with Jordan?

If you went to college in the 80s like I did, you probably remember the bulletin board communication upon which students relied. If you needed a ride to your hometown for the weekend, had a stereo to sell, or were looking for a roommate, you'd tack up a piece of paper with your landline number written several times on little tear-off strips at the bottom. No e-mail address, no cell phone number, no web site.

Somehow we survived without Craigslist, Instagram, Snapchat, and Facebook. We actually (gasp) wrote messages on dry-erase boards on dorm-room doors. Some of us even used pens and paper to compose actual letters we stuffed into envelopes and mailed to friends ... using a postage stamp.

Whether you embrace technology or think, like my husband does, that the internet is the root of all evil, connections can happen with lightning speed now.

I marvel at the way Facebook, for example, can be used to connect people who need each other. One of my friends will post a need or something they have to offer: (*"Our greyhounds grew out of their sweaters. Does anyone know someone who works with greyhound rescue dogs who could use them?"*) Within minutes, I can tag a friend who I know works with rescue dogs who can use the sweaters. Bam, a connection is made and dogs have new sweaters; and two people who didn't previously know each other now have a chance to connect. They already know they both love greyhounds, an instant affinity. Maybe they'll friend each other. If they're intentional affinity builders, they'll invite each other to like a local animal rescue page or some other common page of interest. The beauty of social networking.

## Tell a Story

Sounds like a broken record, I know, but the only way to REALLY get to know someone is to know their stories. People aren't attracted to facts and statistics as much as they are to actual stories. According to Erik Sherman's "The Killer TED Talk Secret for Presentations" (*Inc*; March 31, 2016), it should come as no surprise that, after studying 500 TED talks (short, powerful, and free online talks), researchers found that the most popular ones—the talks that went viral—were the ones that consisted primarily of personal stories. It didn't even matter whether the sound was on or not. At-home audiences liked the story-laden talks better, even if they were just reading the script. Even the talk that Harvard Business School professor Amy Cuddy did about building confidence through body posture, included a story about her feeling like an imposter. Facebook COO Sheryl Sandberg had planned on using statistics in her talk about there being too few women in leadership positions, but a friend convinced her to tell the story of Sandberg's 3-year-old daughter clinging to her, trying to keep her from doing that very TED talk. In fact, 72% of Sandberg's talk was personal stories.

We crave stories because they build affinity. We try to personalize the world around us so that we can better relate to it.

So, whether you're preparing a public presentation or a Facebook post, give of yourself by sharing a personal story.

Your announcements of births, deaths, and marriages garner a lot of engagement on social media because everyone can relate to the joy or sorrow you're sharing. Obituaries include more than just date of birth and date of death because loved ones want to read the STORY of the deceased person's life.

Pictures of giggling babies and cuddly pets resonate broadly, too. Yes, a picture does paint a thousand words, but a good story, no matter how brief, paints a great picture, also.

Don't let the term "story" intimidate you. A story can be a sentence or a book. From personal experience, I've found stories of embarrassing moments and silly mistakes resonate with folks as much as a picture of a newborn Chocolate Lab.

 ACTION

Admit mistakes and share embarrassing moments.

When you talk about yours, it helps others to divulge theirs, too!

Did you ever notice that people's embarrassing moments get an inordinate amount of "likes" on Facebook? It appears from my non-scientific observations of Facebook posts and resulting "likes" and comments that embarrassment is a great affinity-builder. We've all been embarrassed, and it comforts us when we read that other people have, too. The fact is that most people don't publicly share—at least on purpose—the details of their embarrassments. You're not most people. The fact that you've made it this far in the book leads me to believe that you're wanting to be more intentional about your affinity building. So, what's a great way to start? The next time something embarrassing happens, post it as your Facebook status. Or, if you're anti-computer like my husband, be sure to tell several people about your moment of mortification. You'll likely read/hear affinity-laden responses like "I'm glad I'm not the only one that's happened to" or "thanks for the laugh."

Everyone has been embarrassed. Everyone has made mistakes. A sure way to engage people in conversation is to talk about that "oops" moment you've had. Others will jump on that embarrassment bandwagon with tales of their own.

Here's an example of one of my Facebook posts that shows the affinity that can be built by being transparent about life's little mishaps:

**God bless the woman who approached me at Woodman's today to ask if I "meant to wear my skirt that way." Yes, I always prance around the produce aisle with the back half of my floor length skirt caught up into my underwear. #redintheface**

*Oh my! · Yes, God bless her! for your sake! This just made water come out my nose! Trying to make a fashion statement? Haha I think it is called exhibitionism. When it's unintentional I think it is called embarrassing...... Julie I've done this a few times myself! Will tell you the details when I see you! . Jeannie Sorry Betsy, but I just had a laugh out loud moment at your expense! So glad that woman stopped you before you got to the frozen foods isle! Sandy Oops accident...did you have toilet paper streamers too? ·. Tom @Sandy. I thought it, couldn't say it. Mary Ann Talk about the worst embarrassing of moments. You will be telling that story for a very long time!! Sandi OMG. laughing and knowing it could have been me and not you. Bree That is awesome!!!! I hope u were wearing cute undies :) it takes a real woman to post that on Facebook! You're a trooper Julie When my son was 3 yrs. old, he decided to lift my skirt from the back to see what was under it. This wouldn't have been so bad except that I was in one of the front pews at church for a wedding!! Everyone got to see what was under there!. Betsy Leave it to Bree to worry about whether my undies were cute..... Linda If you got it, flaunt it! I'm*

*with Bree on the cute panties--hope they weren't "granny panties"!! . Betsy My con-*
*cerned daughter will be happy to know that I was sporting Victoria's Secrets.......*
*Maurita Betsy, I am laughing out loud!!! Thanks for posting this! I'm sorry to*
*laugh at your misfortune, but it feels great to laugh so hard!. Connie You've got*
*to be kidding!!!!I would die, that is funny!!!!*

## Make it personal

While we're on the topic of sharing stories and getting personal (Affinity Building 101), I'd like to share an easy "opportunity for improvement" in social media posts, specifically as it relates to congratulating each other on birthdays and work anniversaries.

Please indulge me for a few minutes, as I may appear to sound ungrateful. I'm not. I'm a fairly grateful person. However ...

Nothing says "I really don't want to expend a lot of energy on you as a person" more than sending a robotic, automatic LinkedIn message that congratulates people on their work anniversaries. Please, please do not think a "Congratulations on your work anniversary" message that was auto-sent to my LinkedIn page gives the feeling that you even a.) know that it's my work anniversary b.) know where I work or c.) care that it's my work anniversary. If you truly want to wish me a happy work anniversary, include a personal note with your sentiment. When I receive 37 messages on my wall that say "Congratulations on your work anniversary," I'm sorry, but it doesn't give me a warm feeling. The messages, however, that say something like, "Wow, Betsy, I can't believe you've had your own business for 8 years already! I hope you're enjoying it more and more each day!"—those make me feel a connection.

Dare I even go on about birthdays on Facebook? Can you tell that I'm not a fan of receiving 378 posts on my wall that say "Happy Birthday"? Don't get me wrong. I certainly appreciate the 3 seconds that it took (6 seconds for slow typists) to share that sentiment on my wall. I'm just saying that, from an affinity-building perspective, those rote wishes fall short.

Would you ever give a friend or family member a birthday card that simply said, "Happy Birthday," with no picture or other words on it? Probably not.

 ACTION

Personalize your Happy Birthday wishes.

Whether you're buying or making a card, include a photo of a special memory you share with the birthday girl/boy. If you're wishing someone a happy birthday on social media, include a personal wish for them that goes beyond the words "Happy Birthday" to show that you're thinking specifically about them. For example, if your friend Sheila is an avid horse lover, go to google images and enter "Happy Birthday with horses." You will find a plethora of choices for images that will resonate with Sheila. If you're not into using images, at least include a personal wish for Sheila's year ahead: "Happy joy-filled Birthday, Sheila! May you enjoy every day of the coming year." Anything to show that you're spending some time sending her a personal wish and not just the obligatory Facebook-reminded "Happy Birthday."

And, having said all that, I'll still appreciate ANY and EVERY birthday wish I receive, personalized or not.

## Social Media Advertising and Affinity

It's no surprise that advertisers and companies have been using the affinity concept for years to capture the attention of the "right" audiences. Take, for example, Facebook. Mark Z. and his team enable their advertisers to exclude users by age affinities, religious affinities, sports team affinities, and even ethnic affinities. They limit which users see their material.

Since Facebook doesn't even require us to specify our race, you might wonder how they know our ethnicity. They know because of good guesses they make based on our other affinities. Facebook, and other advertisers, collect activity data and then assign us an ethnic affinity. Basically, they look at our preference for certain stories, events, and what type of people/organizations we like, and they decide on how those preferences coincide with certain ethnic groups and certain mindsets.

This stuff isn't rocket science ... but, it's definitely a science. Each time you "like" something, post something, open a link to read an article, you are making an affinity statement about yourself. Before you click and before you post, be sure it's a statement you want to make.

# 6

## The Unintended, Undesirable Consequences Of Affinities

*As we are, so we associate. The good, by affinity, seek the good;*
*the vile, by affinity, the vile.*

– RALPH WALDO EMERSON

I WOULD BE remiss if I didn't spend some time cautioning you about some unintended—and often undesirable—consequences of affinity building.

## The Wrong Motivation

It makes sense that humans are drawn to others who are "like" them. Sadly, though, that attraction is what often prevents us from wanting to seek out others who are "less like" us. The whole motivation for becoming an intentional affinity builder should not be, "I want to find people who are like me." Instead, it should be "I want to find similarities between others and myself and build on those to get to know others more fully." If your motivation is the former, you're cheating yourself out of opportunities to build relationships with people who are very unlike you ... and who have a lot to offer.

> *Silence fell over the group like a blanket extinguishing a fire. It was the awkward quiet of people who don't know each other that well....who still feel obligated to fill the spaces between them. Corrine, Leslie, and Jane were held together by the flimsiest of threads. They had nothing in common beyond nationality. In New York, they might never have met. As a group, they manufactured fun, but there was a sense that they were all settling for one another's company.* (excerpt from *You Are One of Them*, by Elliott Holt)

That affinity that seems so obvious and important, like the color of our skin or nationality, can really be a "flimsy thread." Don't settle for superficial affinities.

## Affinity Biases

Our close associations with people and groups with whom we are bonded can create ethical blind spots. In their book *Blind Spots,* business professors Max H. Bazerman and Ann E. Tenbrunsel explain that research shows that people are intuitively most comfortable doing favors for those with whom we identify—that is, with people who are a lot like us (with whom we have an affinity). Psychologists call this phenomenon *in-group favoritism.* In particular, we tend to be biased toward those who share our alma mater, religion, gender, or race.

Since we have a tendency to show subconscious favoritism to people in our affinity circle, we run a risk of unintentionally discriminating against those outside our circle. An equally disturbing side-effect of affinity is that we tend to more easily overlook the wrongdoing of people in our affinity circle.

Nowhere is this concept more evident than in sports and politics. We vote for a specific candidate because s/he represents the party with which we have the most affinity. When s/he does or says something while in office that would otherwise have disturbed us, we rationalize it because we are blinded by our affinity with that person and party. Sound familiar?

A referee calls pass interference against one of "our" team members; we flail our arms and yell at the TV about how stupid and wrong that call is. We don't even wait for the replay; we have such a strong affinity with our team that we're sure they did nothing wrong. Sound familiar?

So, how can we correct some of the lopsided effects of affinity? In my experience, it helps to put ourselves in the place of those outside my affinity group (Chicago Bears fans, for example … sorry, couldn't resist).

First of all, I need to recognize that, while people might be outside a certain affinity group (Bears fans vs. Packers fans), there are a WHOLE lot of things people in those two groups have in common. Considering the Venn diagram in the beginning of this book, if I completed a diagram with a Bears fan, there would be plenty of commonalities in the intersection. I do, in fact, have some dear friends and family with the Bears-fan affliction. We love each other despite our differences in sports loyalties.

Sports analogies can be shallow, so let's dive deeper. What about people who are in a different religious affinity circle than we are? If you're a Christian or a Jew, are you willing to seek the intersections in the Venn diagram with Muslims and atheists? No matter the difference in affinity, we will never overcome our biases by spending more time focusing on differences than on similarities.

Second, we need to put ourselves in "the shoes of" people outside our affinity group. Let's use the example of a pass interference call in a Packers/Bears game. If the ref is calling the penalty on a Packers player, my first inclination is to assume the ref may be wrong. Because I'm aware of my "in-group favoritism," I now ask myself, "If that call were made on a Bears player, would I think it was correct?" I do the same with politics.

When a politician I didn't vote for takes a stand on an issue, I ask, "How would I feel if 'my side' were taking that stand? Would I feel just as upset about it, or would I embrace it?" Test yourself during the next State of the State or State of the Union address. When you're cheering or jeering, examine how you would be reacting if the "other side" were delivering the same address.

Recognize your biases. Then be willing to see things from the point of view of someone in a different affinity group.

## Blue Lies

When we're closely connected to a person or group, we often overlook the things about them that irritate us. We sometimes even take that blanket acceptance to an unhealthy extreme—we start believing, or at least accepting, lies that those in our affinity group tell. And sometimes those lies actually serve to bond us closer. Scientists have a name for this phenomenon: blue lies.

Blue lies, according to Jeremy Adam Smith in *Scientific American* (March 27, 2017) are a very particular form of deception that can build solidarity within groups. Smith uses President Trump and his followers as an illustration. Why is it that, even when many of Trump's statements have been proven false, many of his supporters seem to keep believing him or making excuses for his lies?

Smith's article is fascinating to me; check out this excerpt:

*Journalists and researchers have suggested many answers, from hyperbiased, segmented media to simple ignorance on the part of GOP voters. But there is another explanation that no one seems to have entertained. It is that Trump is telling "blue" lies — a psychologist's term for falsehoods, told on behalf of a group, that can actually strengthen the bonds among the members of that group.*

*Children start to tell selfish lies at about age three, as they discover adults cannot read their minds: I didn't steal that toy, Daddy said I could, He hit me first. At around age seven, they begin to tell white lies motivated by feelings of empathy and compassion: That's a good draw-ing, I love socks for Christmas, You're funny.*

*Blue lies are a different category altogether, simultaneously selfish and beneficial to others — but only to those who belong to your group. As University of Toronto psychologist Kang Lee explained, blue lies fall in between generous white lies and selfish "black" ones. "You can tell a blue lie against another group," he said, which makes it simultaneously self-less and self-serving. "For example, you can lie about your team's cheat-ing in a game, which is antisocial, but helps your team."*

In a 2008 study of seven, nine, and eleven-year-old children — the first of its kind — Lee and colleagues found that children become more likely to endorse and tell blue lies as they grow older. For example, given an opportunity to lie to an interviewer about rule-breaking in the selec-tion process of a school chess team, many were quite willing to do so, older kids more than younger ones. The children telling this lie didn't stand to selfishly benefit; they were doing it on behalf of their school. This line of research finds that black lies drive people apart, white lies draw them together, and blue lies pull some people together while driv-ing others away.

Bottom line: Be aware of how your ties with an affinity group affect your ability to be objective. Resist the temptation to tell or accept lies just because of your bond. Lies hurt people. And the key to building affinity is CARING about people, ALL people—so there is never a healthy place for lies.

## When Affinities Conflict

External Conflict: a conflict between two affinity groups or concepts

Internal Conflict: a conflict among members or concepts within an affinity group

So what happens when different affinity groups we're in are in conflict? For example, what if you're in the "Pro Life" affinity group but you're also in the "Democrat" group? Or what if you're a health food advocate with a penchant for fast-food French fries? Some would call these dual affinities hypocrisies. But, let's face it—there are very few affinities that are pure and without overlap.

These overlaps and conflicts in our affinity groups lead to *cognitive dissonance*, the fancy psychological term for "these contradictions don't feel right." The woman picketing in front of an abortion clinic and handing out Hillary Clinton election flyers in the same day has some emotional balancing to do. She has to determine whether the qualities/policies she likes about Hillary Clinton outweigh her fervent desire to end abortion.

It's a fascinating, albeit often subconscious, exercise that accompanies these affinity "solutions." Sometimes the dissonance is overcome by redefining or relabeling our affinity group. For example, I was a huge Michael Jackson fan in the 1980's—I was thrilled with "Thriller" along with most of the world. While I continued to appreciate and enjoy Jackson's amazing singing and dancing talent, I became embarrassed in the 90's to admit that I was a "fan." So I basically pulled myself out of the "Michael Jackson Fan" affinity group and moved into the group that still appreciated his talent but pitied the sad state of his life.

## Affinity doesn't always equal participation

Don't mistake "showing an interest" in another person's hobbies, passions, or experiences as having an affinity. For example, the president at the college where I worked was an avid race car driver. As much as that fact intrigued me about him, I couldn't pretend to have an affinity for race car driving.

On the other hand if I truly wanted to build an affinity with this man, I could have worked on learning more about the sport of racing, perhaps even trying to experience it myself. Does that mean I would have automatically bonded with the sport? Absolutely not. Chances are I would have built an appreciation for the sport but not a passion, interest, or even much of an understanding. Affinities cannot be forced; they can be worked on and nurtured, but cannot be manufactured.

Don't let relationships depend only on obvious affinities, such as your sex or race or the fact that you belong to the same gym.

While I understand the need for professional and social groups to create an identity based on a specific characteristic (e.g. your college alumni association), I think it's a shame people cling to those affinities to the exclusion of others. By the same token, don't let your relationship with someone stop ONLY at your affinities/intersections with them. If you have bonded with someone because you both play the piano, don't let music be the only thing you talk about. Intersections may draw us to certain people; it's how we build on those intersections that creates meaningful relationships.

Having said that, however, there will likely be people in our lives with whom we bond only because of one or two important things we have in common. Your workout partner at the gym may always stay only your "gym buddy." If they drop their gym membership, you may never see them again. That's life. There's no need to force friendship, but if you're seeking to build meaningful relationships, you'll need to look beyond the intersections that brought you together.

The United States is commonly called "The Melting Pot." Yes, it's true that we are rich in assimilated diversity. But "melting pot" implies that we are to give up our differences to "melt" into one culture. From an affinity perspective, this is a myth. The Venn diagram approach shows that the whole circles representing each individual do not change when they intersect; on the contrary, the circle is only enhanced as a portion of another circle intersects it with commonalities.

## Stereotypes

The most obvious drawback of the affinity concept is the false assumption that everyone in a certain group feels/acts the same way. Don't judge people by their affinity groups. These prejudices and stereotypes are what lead to misunderstandings, missed opportunities for relationships, and clashes within and between groups.

I went through a painful divorce, and I was a single mother for a few years. Does that mean I know and can relate to what all other single mothers are feeling and experiencing? Of course not. But, somehow, we have a tendency to think that, because we've experienced something, everyone else will experience it the same way.

Just because you're part of a family or employment group or church doesn't mean you feel an affinity with the others in those groups. On the contrary, you may feel like the proverbial "fish out of water" and prefer not to be viewed as a member of certain groups. When we let a group define us, we risk being stereotyped.

## Affinity can lead to complacency

"You always hurt the one you love." A catchy lyric, yes, but it can also become a truism of affinity if we're not careful. Don't take people for granted because they have a lot in common with you; and don't assume because you have one thing in common that you have a "tight" bond. You and a guy you meet at a party may both be UCLA alums; that doesn't make you best friends or even buddies. It's simply one thing you can use as a starting point for further conversation and relationship building, if you desire.

# 7

## So What? Values Of Affinity Building

*An hour spent drinking tea is the hour when the prince and the peasant share thoughts and ready themselves for the commonalities and woes of their separate lives.*

−OLD PROVERB

THIS CHAPTER MAY seem repetitive as I re-cap the reasons I'm such a promoter of affinity building. Since repetition is a key to attaching ideas to our brain, read this chapter with an eye for the end result of *why* it's so important to become intentional about building affinity.

### Affinities affect our decisions

People make decisions—large and small—based on who/what they have an affinity for/with. I worship at a certain church because I have a strong affinity with a certain denomination; I play on-line word games because I have a strong affinity for the English language (and I love a good game!); I eat at certain restaurants because my affinity for the owners trumps the fact that their food isn't my favorite, etc.

Some affinities "count" more than others, and, therefore, have a larger influence on human behavior. Our affinity group influences play a larger role in our decisions, actions, and feelings than we realize. A tongue-in-cheek list going around on social media of "Things that all Southern People Understand" includes: "You know that no matter where you are in the world, if you run into a fellow Southerner, you've got a true friend in them." That says a lot about the affinity of geography and culture, doesn't it?

Think back to the 2008 U.S. Presidential election. One of the greatest "affinity score" examples happened that year. Disclaimer: this observation is mine only and not intended to be "political fact."

General Colin Powell has always been one of my political, social, and intellectual heroes. His compassionate conservative values align closely with mine. Imagine my surprise when General Powell supported Barack Obama in the 2008 presidential election. The only logical explanation I could see for that uncharacteristic move was that the value General Powell placed on his African American affinity was higher than the value of his affinity for political conservatism.

This affinity stuff is powerful, and it's often subconscious.

## Affinity creates a sense of belonging

People long to belong. It's part of the human condition.

The cool thing about being in an affinity group is that once you're in it, you'll always have a certain bond with fellow group members, even if you move out of the group. Just because we move beyond the group doesn't mean we can't remember. I'll always, for example, have an understanding of what it's like to be a single mother, even though I'm not in that group anymore.

Being in an affinity group (or being a past member) doesn't mean that you view things, feel things, or experience things in the same way as fellow group members. There are varying degrees of affinity. Packers fans, for example, come in a wide variety, ranging from the green-and-gold-painted, cheesehead–sporting half-naked bizarros you see on TV to the casual viewer who catches a game once in a while or wears an Aaron Rodgers jersey to work on casual Fridays. I fall somewhere in between (I may or may not have sported a cheesehead while eating deep-fried cheese curds during a Packers game).

The sense of belonging to an affinity group is not an end in itself. Because we feel we *belong* to a group, we are inspired to bond with fellow group members. A consequence of this bonding is that we often get to know each other better. Being intentional about sharing stories—inside and outside of our affinity group—is a great way to build on the foundation started by the initial affinity. For example, no matter where Packers fans are on the "fanatic" spectrum, they all can share at least one memory about a certain Packers game. Maybe it was the Ice Bowl, maybe it was a Super Bowl, or maybe it was a game against one of our biggest rivals.

Here's a story I wrote that was included in Steve Rose's *Pea Soup for the Packer Heart (2010):*

*It was a Sunday in 1982, and the Green Bay Packers were playing the Chicago Bears. My parents were at the Mayo Clinic dealing with some of my dad's many health issues. My best friend Dawn and I (both of us 16) were watching the game because pretty much everybody watched the Packers/Bears match-up. Well, this was the game (you'll remember it if you're a Packers fan over age 35) in which Packers kicker Chester Marcol miraculously ended up with his blocked field goal and blindly stumbled to the goal line with it, sealing a victory.*

*We and thousands of Packers fans erupted with hooting and hollering. Dawn and I spilled out into our driveway and joined some of the neighbor guys who had been watching at their house. Following the celebration, I invited the guys to join Dawn and me for a game of pool in our basement. We played a lively game, re-hashing the Packers victory. When we finished, my neighbor Tim and I rolled the remaining balls into the pockets to clear the table. Neither of us realized that we were both rolling a ball (he the purple four ball) very hard toward each other. The balls collided, and the purple ball flew straight at my face, smashing my teeth.*

*Shocked and holding pieces of my teeth, I asked Dawn to call a friend's mother who was a nurse. I didn't want to trouble Mom and Dad, given the stress they were already under with my dad's health. Taking Tylenol and calling the dentist was the nurse's suggestion. I don't need to tell you how mortifying it was for a teen-aged girl to be missing most of two front teeth ... never mind that it hurt a bit. All I could think about was what I looked like (think hillbilly) and how much it was going to cost. My family struggled financially, especially because of all my dad's hospital bills, and now this.*

*I don't know how we managed to pay for it, but the ordeal led to a root canal (the pretty purple ball had damaged my roots) and crowns. First there were temporary crowns, one of which fell off an hour before a Pom-Pon routine, in which I was in the front row. Missing part of my front tooth (think Hillbilly again), I somehow managed to smile with my mouth closed the whole time.*

*Purple is a Vikings color, but I still think of the Packers every time I see the purple four ball on a pool table.*

Whether you're a Packers fan or not, some parts of that story may resonate with you. Maybe you've had a "pool table mishap." Maybe you've endured a root canal. Maybe you can relate to not wanting to add to your family's financial hardships. Maybe you've been to the Mayo Clinic.

The more background and detail a personal story has, the more likely it is to strike a chord with others.

## Affinities provide comfort

*Praise be to the God and Father of our Lord Jesus Christ, the Father of compassion and the God of all comfort, who comforts us in all our troubles, so that we can comfort those in any trouble with the comfort we ourselves receive from God.*

*- 2 Corinthians 1:3-4 (New International Version of the Holy Bible)*

As I've said before, humans didn't create affinity building—God did. He comforts us not just so we will be comforted, but so *we can comfort others.* I love this!

Julie Cantrell's novel *The Feathered Bone (2016, chapter 24))* includes a stunning and beautiful example of this, as the main character (a social worker whose daughter died by suicide a year earlier) is called upon to provide comfort to a pregnant young wife who just lost her husband to suicide:

*I've been on calls with Jay many times, but not since Ellie took her own life....not since I wrapped my hands around my own ears and sobbed, wanting death to take me away. But now that I know this walk, I begin by taking off my official social worker hat and being present as nothing more than a survivor. I show my own scars, something my license would never allow.*

*"My daughter committed suicide," I say softly. "Almost a year ago. She was barely 14. I was alone when I found her."*

*She may not hear what I'm saying, but I trust the right words will find their way to her at the right time; that's all I can do.*

*"The night she died I was home with her. I walked into her room. She was on her bed just lying there. She used a gun, too."*

*I continue, detail after detail, letting her know that not only do I care, but I understand. I've been there. I'm still there.*

*When I say, "She was my only child," the woman stops rocking and moaning, and pulls her hands away from her head.*

*As she looks at me I say, "You will get through this. I promise. I'm here to help you. Lots of people are here to help you."*

*She reaches for my hand. I repeat this message in various ways again and again. It finally begins to sink in. Twenty minutes later she crawls out of the closet and leans against the bedroom wall. Her arms curl tight around her belly. Her eyes connect with mine, as if I'm all she has to believe in anymore.*

*"Stay with me," she says.*

*The fact that I'm still here, that I somehow survived my daughter's suicide is enough to get her to the next inhale.*

Wow. That pretty much says it all. Affinity provides comfort ... but we must be intentional. We must choose to reach out to comfort those who are hurting in ways we ourselves have hurt.

I can't stress enough how important it is to be transparent—both in our triumphs and in our sorrows—so others know how to come alongside us. We have to let people know when we need comfort, and we need to respond when we have comfort to give.

When we lost Zach to his drug addiction, we felt strongly about being transparent in his obituary. Sadly, so many obituaries fail to mention the cause of death because loved ones are ashamed. There is NOTHING to be ashamed of. In fact I feel that omitting suicide, overdose, or other causes of death that may be uncomfortable to share sends the wrong message. It says there's something to be embarrassed about, something that shouldn't be admitted or talked about. On the contrary, suicide and addiction NEED to be talked about. If Zach had died of cancer, we would have shared that he died of cancer. Why, then, would we not share that he died of a drug overdose that stemmed from his addiction?

It's in sharing that we build affinity. It's in sharing that we ask for comfort. It's in sharing that we provide comfort.

Here are some excerpts from Zach's obituary:

**Zachary B. Rozelle**

Our precious Zach's story sounds far too common and familiar lately. On October 5th, Zach died of an accidental heroin overdose. We share his story in the hope that it might save others from the incredible heartache we are experiencing.

Zach was born on April 25, 1986 and was baptized at Bethany Lutheran in Appleton and confirmed at St. Paul, where his special verse was "God is our refuge and strength, an ever-present help in trouble"

-Psalm 46:1. He graduated from Fox Valley Lutheran in 2005 and went on to carry on his grandfather and father's legacy at Rozelle Construction.

His heart was as big as his beard, and his smile and laugh would light up a room. There was never a question where Zach's heart was—he was real. He was kind. He was generous. He loved eggs benedict, prime rib, techno music, and glow sticks. He struggled with anxiety.

Zach loved spending weekends at the deer shack with family, snorkeling with his dad and soaking in the beauty of Door County. Zach took amazing photographs.

He was a big movie buff and could rehash the story line from every movie he ever saw. *Family Guy* was his guilty pleasure and he would have rather pierced his own lip than miss the new episodes on Sunday nights.

Zach had a passion for riding motorcycles, and he was quite the poi ball expert. He was proud of his gun collection, and loved his little dog Roo.

An addict is fighting an uphill battle. As loved ones, we intervene and do what we can to show tough love and help them out of their agony.

If you are struggling, or know someone who is – please do not wait until it is too late. At Zach's funeral, we will be reminded that the Lord asks us to lay down your burdens, lay down your shame, all who are broken, lift up your face. Oh wanderer come home, you're not too far. So lay down your hurt, lay down your heart, and come to Him as you are. (Come as You Are; Crowder 2014).

In lieu of flowers, a memorial fund is being set up in Zach's memory.

Do not be silent. Winnebago Crisis Center 920-233-7707 Outagamie Crisis Center 920-722-7707.

The outpouring of love and comfort was overwhelming. People who didn't know us reached out because they had experienced the loss of a loved one through addiction. People reach out to us now when they're going through the pain of loving someone who is battling addiction. We are in an ever-growing affinity intersection of lives touched by the horrors of addiction.

We can be consoled by anyone who has love to give; those with love and the affinity of the grief we bear provide comfort in a unique way. I challenge you to reach out to those whose grief and trials you've experienced. Be reminded that we all experience sadness and grief differently, so don't take the "I know what you're going through" literally. But, having an idea of what someone is experiencing gives us a great foundation for comforting them.

## Affinity builds resiliency

Share stories of your childhood with family members.

There's another version of my "share stories" suggestion again. Yes, it's important enough to keep repeating it. If you've taken nothing else away from this book, please take the idea of sharing your stories!

Share stories of your childhood with your kids, nieces/nephews, and friends' children. This sounds basic. Haven't we all heard the, "I walked 5 miles to school every day barefoot" stories?

In my research about the benefits of what I call affinity building, I was intrigued and so pleased to learn that research has shown a link between a sense of self control over life/self-esteem and the amount we know about our family's history.

*"This Life"* appears monthly in *Sunday Styles.* This article is adapted from Bruce Feiler's 2013 book, *"The Secrets of Happy Families: How to Improve Your Morning, Rethink Family Dinner, Fight Smart, Go Out and Play, and Much More."* The following excerpt is lengthy, but I find it so helpful in understanding the crucial nature of affinity-building within families.

*I hit the breaking point as a parent a few years ago. It was the week of my extended family's annual gathering in August, and we were struggling with assorted crises. My parents were aging; my wife and I were straining under the chaos of young children; my sister was bracing to prepare her preteens for bullying, sex and cyberstalking.*

*Sure enough, one night all the tensions boiled over. At dinner, I noticed my nephew texting under the table. I knew I shouldn't say anything, but I couldn't help myself and asked him to stop.*

*Ka-boom! My sister snapped at me to not discipline her child. My dad pointed out that my girls were the ones balancing spoons on their noses. My mom said none of the grandchildren had manners. Within minutes, everyone had fled to separate corners.*

*Later, my dad called me to his bedside. There was a palpable sense of fear I couldn't remember hearing before.*

*"Our family's falling apart," he said.*

*"No it's not," I said instinctively. "It's stronger than ever."*

*But lying in bed afterward, I began to wonder: Was he right? What is the secret sauce that holds a family together? What are the ingredients that make some families effective, resilient, happy?*

*It turns out to be an astonishingly good time to ask that question. The last few years have seen stunning breakthroughs in knowledge about how to make families, along with other groups, work more effectively.*

*Myth-shattering research has reshaped our understanding of dinnertime, discipline and difficult conversations. Trendsetting programs from Silicon Valley and the military have introduced techniques for making teams function better.*

*The only problem: most of that knowledge remains ghettoized in these subcultures, hidden from the parents who need it most. I spent the last few years trying to uncover that information, meeting families, scholars and experts ranging from peace negotiators to online game designers to Warren Buffett's bankers.*

*After a while, a surprising theme emerged. The single most important thing you can do for your family may be the simplest of all: develop a strong family narrative.*

*I first heard this idea from Marshall Duke, a colorful psychologist at Emory University. In the mid-1990s, Dr. Duke was asked to help explore myth and ritual in American families.*

*"There was a lot of research at the time into the dissipation of the family," he told me at his home in suburban Atlanta. "But we were more interested in what families could do to counteract those forces."*

*Around that time, Dr. Duke's wife, Sara, a psychologist who works with children with learning disabilities, noticed something about her students.*

*"The ones who know a lot about their families tend to do better when they face challenges," she said.*

*Her husband was intrigued, and along with a colleague, Robyn Fivush, set out to test her hypothesis. They developed a measure called the "Do You Know?" scale that asked children to answer 20 questions.*

***Examples included: Do you know where your grandparents grew up? Do you know where your mom and dad went to high school? Do you know where your parents met? Do you know an illness or***

*something really terrible that happened in your family? Do you know the story of your birth?*

Dr. Duke and Dr. Fivush asked those questions of four dozen families in the summer of 2001, and taped several of their dinner table conversations. They then compared the children's results to a battery of psychological tests the children had taken, and reached an overwhelming conclusion. The more children knew about their family's history, the stronger their sense of control over their lives, the higher their self-esteem and the more successfully they believed their families functioned. The "Do You Know?" scale turned out to be the best single predictor of children's emotional health and happiness.

"We were blown away," Dr. Duke said.

And then something unexpected happened. Two months later was Sept. 11. As citizens, Dr. Duke and Dr. Fivush were horrified like everyone else, but as psychologists, they knew they had been given a rare opportunity: though the families they studied had not been directly affected by the events, all the children had experienced the same national trauma at the same time. The researchers went back and reassessed the children.

"Once again," Dr. Duke said, "the ones who knew more about their families proved to be more resilient, meaning they could moderate the effects of stress."

Why does knowing where your grandmother went to school help a child overcome something as minor as a skinned knee or as major as a terrorist attack?

"The answers have to do with a child's sense of being part of a larger family," Dr. Duke said.

Psychologists have found that every family has a unifying narrative, he explained, and those narratives take one of three shapes.

First, the ascending family narrative: "Son, when we came to this country, we had nothing. Our family worked. We opened a store. Your grandfather went to high school. Your father went to college. And now you. ..."

*Second is the descending narrative: "Sweetheart, we used to have it all. Then we lost everything."*

*"The most healthful narrative," Dr. Duke continued, "is the third one. It's called the oscillating family narrative: 'Dear, let me tell you, we've had ups and downs in our family. We built a family business. Your grandfather was a pillar of the community. Your mother was on the board of the hospital. But we also had setbacks. You had an uncle who was once arrested. We had a house burn down. Your father lost a job. But no matter what happened, we always stuck together as a family.' "*

*Dr. Duke said that children who have the most self-confidence have what he and Dr. Fivush call a strong "intergenerational self." They know they belong to something bigger than themselves.*

*Leaders in other fields have found similar results. Many groups use what sociologists call sense-making, the building of a narrative that explains what the group is about.*

*Jim Collins, a management expert and author of "Good to Great," told me that successful human enterprises of any kind, from companies to countries, go out of their way to capture their core identity. In Mr. Collins's terms, they "preserve core, while stimulating progress." The same applies to families, he said.*

*Mr. Collins recommended that families create a mission statement similar to the ones companies and other organizations use to identify their core values.*

*. . . Dr. Duke recommended that parents pursue similar activities with their children. Any number of occasions work to convey this sense of history: holidays, vacations, big family get-togethers, even a ride to the mall. The hokier the family's tradition, he said, the more likely it is to be passed down. He mentioned his family's custom of hiding frozen turkeys and canned pumpkin in the bushes during Thanksgiving so grandchildren would have to "hunt for their supper," like the Pilgrims.*

*"These traditions become part of your family," Dr. Duke said.*

*Decades of research have shown that most happy families communicate effectively. But talking doesn't mean simply "talking through problems," as important as that is. Talking also means telling a positive story about yourselves. When faced with a challenge, happy families, like happy people, just add a new chapter to their life story that shows them overcoming the hardship. This skill is particularly important for children, whose identity tends to get locked in during adolescence.*

***The bottom line: if you want a happier family, create, refine and retell the story of your family's positive moments and your ability to bounce back from the difficult ones. That act alone may increase the odds that your family will thrive for many generations to come. (Bruce Feiler, 2013)***

 ACTION

Create a family mission statement.

Identify your family's core values, and put them in writing. Use this exercise as a way to brainstorm about why these values are important and about how previous generations of your family demonstrated them.

It's clear that building family cohesiveness will help the next generation of children in a multitude of ways. As I look forward to grandchildren, I'm already brainstorming about which stories to share with them and how to lead a "mission statement" session for our family.

## Affinity builds team cohesion

*On the railroad trains, all the passengers together were a community, called by a shared moral understanding to sacrifice for each other. But if, as we now seem to think there are no other passengers, there is no community. And if there is no community, we*

*can do what we like, not just on the roads but everywhere. The*
*illusion that we travel life alone is ruining us all.*

*– AUTHOR STEPHEN L. CARTER*

If you've ever been in charge of a team or group, you know that one of
the keys to success is building cohesion among group members. That's
Affinity 101, right?

We can learn a lot from the military about team building, as cohesion is often a matter of life or death.

Here's more from *Bruce Feiler's "The Secrets of Happy Families: How to
Improve Your Morning, Rethink Family Dinner, Fight Smart, Go Out and Play,
and Much More."*

*The military has also found that teaching recruits about the history of
their service increases their camaraderie and ability to bond more closely
with their unit.*

*Cmdr. David G. Smith is the chairman of the department of leader-
ship, ethics and law at the Naval Academy and an expert in unit cohesion, the Pentagon's term for group morale. Until recently, the military
taught unit cohesion by "dehumanizing" individuals, Commander Smith
said. Think of the bullying drill sergeants in "Full Metal Jacket" or "An
Officer and a Gentleman."*

*But these days the military spends more time building up identity
through communal activities. At the Naval Academy, Commander Smith
advises graduating seniors to take incoming freshmen (or plebes) on
history-building exercises, like going to the cemetery to pay tribute to the first
naval aviator or visiting the original B-1 aircraft on display on campus.*

"Communal activities" now trump "dehumanizing" techniques for a
reason. The bond of building community creates an "all for one and

one for all" mindset. Yes, each individual is important, but the group is equally important. That's an essential foundation of affinity building, whether it's in a family, a work group, sports team, or military platoon.

## Affinities build trust and pride

*As much as I hated the Corps in basic, I discovered that unlike my old man, it did give me some skills to survive by. And something I'd felt only when I spent time with Ernie: a sense of pride. Not necessarily American pride, but pride in belonging to the Marines. They wanted me. Was that so bad? It was not so much the Corps as it was the guys I met and trained with. I got a whole slew of brothers when I joined up, with only a few of them being assholes like in any family. I was worth something to them. They were worth something to me. That was the secret of survival.* –Mary Relindes Ellis' character Jimmy Lucas, talking about his new role as a marine in the novel *The Turtle Warrior* (2004, p. 188)

The military is a great example of how being part of a group creates a common bond. But you don't have to become a Marine to be a part of a special group.

 ACTION

| Join a club. |
| --- |

The camaraderie builds trust and pride.

Trust is earned. It's usually earned only after getting to know someone. Whether the club you join is an "official" club like Rotary or a Quilting Guild, or whether it's an unofficial one like a group of moms having playdates with their children, the time spent with fellow members leads to trust building. Interestingly, even when we don't know all members of a club, we often trust them simply because they belong to the same club (caution from Chapter Six: not all club members deserve our trust).

A Facebook friend's post illustrates this blind trust we often have of people in "our club":

*Had a great time with friend Leslie at the Quilt Expo in Madison today. Best moment: Leslie tried to pay for a purchase with her credit card. Vendor didn't take plastic, but said, 'Why don't you just mail me a check?' We both stood, with our mouths open for awhile........could it be that people with common interests trust each other?*

As a Rotarian, I have an invitation to attend a Rotary meeting anywhere in the world. I'm welcomed with open arms and trusted as someone who has committed to live by the same values as Rotarians worldwide. It's more than trust, though; it's pride. I'm proud to be a part of this amazing organization that puts "service above self."

# 8

---

## Exercises To Strengthen Your Affinity Muscles

*Affinity building is prolific, but rarely is it deliberate or intentional.*

– BETSY ROZELLE

PRACTICE, PRACTICE, PRACTICE. Like any skill, affinity-building requires practice. In addition to the 33 action steps I gave you to practice, here are a couple of the affinity-building exercises I use with clients.

## Exercise 1: I thought I knew you

This first exercise is ideal for groups of people who already know each other. I ask members to pair up with someone they feel they know pretty well. I then instruct them to complete the 6 questions as if they were the person with whom they're paired. So, if I'm paired with Jane Doe,

I'd fill in Jane Doe for the name, complete #2 with what Jane's father does/did for a living, etc. There is NO TALKING allowed during this exercise.

## AFFINITY BUILDING EXERCISE
### I thought I knew you

**Fill in the following blanks as if you were the other person.**

1. Name _____.
2. What my father does/did for a living _____.
3. Graduated from _____ High School.
4. Other than work, one of the biggest challenges
   in my life right now is _____.
5. I have _____ children and _____ pets.
6. I have a collection of _____.
7. When I was in high school, my career goal was to be
   a _____.

Given that these pairs are often co-workers who spend eight hours a day together and often eat lunch side-by-side, you would think they would know some of these basic things about each other, right? Wrong. Typically, most people in the room get fewer than half of the answers correct. Rarely will anyone have all the answers right. Why? Because we don't tend to ask a lot of personal questions in the workplace or on teams; and we rarely share a lot of personal information about ourselves. There is always SO MUCH more to learn about people we see regularly, and this exercise shows a sampling of that.

The one time I can remember when both people in a pair got all but one answer correct is when 2 maintenance workers were paired with each other. I asked, "So, why do you think you got so many answers right?" Their reply: "We talk a lot and ask a lot of questions." Makes sense. The simple act of talking and sharing builds rapport like nothing else. True, we're not always in work or team situations that are conducive for talking a lot; that's what lunch breaks are for. One of the reasons to NOT eat lunch alone at your desk is that it doesn't allow you to get to know your co-workers better.

As with any affinity-building exercise I do, the purpose isn't to get the answers right. The purpose is to get people talking. The conversations that are sparked when the pairs share the correct answers with each other are golden. Affinity is built on sharing, and people often need a jumpstart like these 6 simple questions.

## Exercise 2: The Affinity Pyramid

My mother-in-law (Mooie) and I were in the ICU waiting room while my father-in-law was undergoing heart-valve surgery. We were speaking in hushed tones because there was an elderly woman on the other side of the room, probably also waiting for a loved one in surgery.

"Tell me about this book you're writing," Mooie said. "What do you mean by *affinity*?"

First, I explained that affinity is the connection between people, based on common experiences, passions, and interests. "I'm writing this book as a training tool," I went on, "because the ability to discover and develop those connections is so important, and I want to help people get better at it."

I took out my pencil and paper to explain one of my affinity-building exercises.

"I created this Affinity Pyramid as one way to help people get to know each other better," I explained, as I drew a blank pyramid.

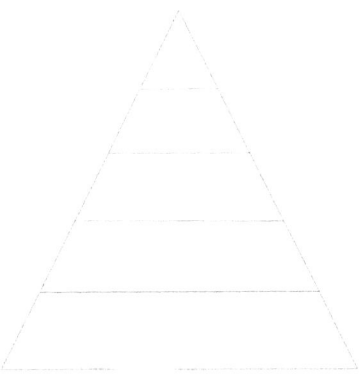

"You see how each level of the pyramid gets smaller? Well, let's say the bottom level represents something you and I have in common with a large number of people ... how about the fact that we're sports fans?" I asked as I filled in the bottom level.

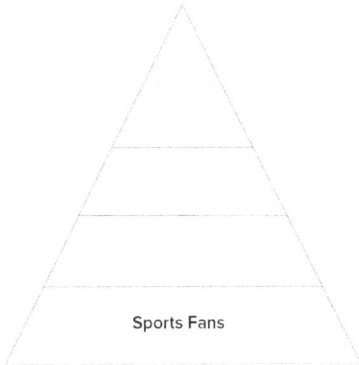

Sports Fans

I continued, "As we move up the pyramid, let's fill it in with something we have in common with fewer people, and so on as we move upward. Ultimately, our goal is to find something that we have in common with a relatively small number of people; in other words, something kind of exclusive. That would make it a really special affinity because it's like we're in a special club together that only a limited number of people are in. Does that make sense?"

"Yeah," Mooie said. "So where would you put that we are Packers fans?"

"Perfect, you get the idea. I would say the next level up on the pyramid would be "NFL Football Fans," I said as I filled in the next level. There's still a very large number of people in that group. Then the Packers fans distinction would be the next level up, as that group is smaller (and, of course, better)," I joked, as I filled in the third level.

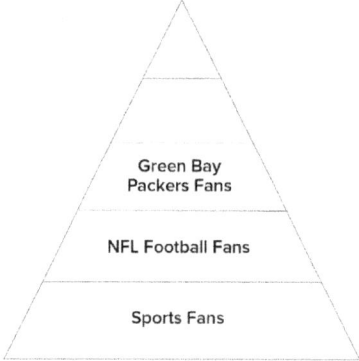

On a roll, I went on to fill in the next level. "Of all the Packers fans in the world, a relatively small number of them have actually experienced a game at Lambeau Field. These are those of us fortunate enough to have breathed in the beer-tinged aroma of brats, heard the crash of the shoulder pads, and felt the electricity of an in-person Lambeau experience. You see how each level up gets smaller and smaller because of the exclusivity?" Mooie's enthusiastic nod told me she was tracking with me.

With only one level left to fill in, I said, "The very pinnacle of this pyramid, which I don't have in common with you, is that you attended the Ice Bowl."

As I put pencil to paper to fill in "Ice Bowl" at the top, the elderly woman across the room jumped up and said, "I was at the Ice Bowl!"

Wow. I couldn't have scripted that affinity lesson any better if I had tried! This woman (we learned her name was Eleanor) bounded over to us—apparently she had been listening to our hushed voices—and introduced herself. She and Mooie excitedly shared their Ice Bowl experience and went on to learn they grew up within 20 miles of each other. Both of them had husbands currently undergoing heart surgery. Needless to say, their initial bond of a very cold and memorable football game was the starting point for a lot of great conversation and even comfort.

The most important part of this exercise is not completing the pyramid. It's in the questions and conversations that take place while trying to fill in levels of the pyramid. It's in the asking of the questions ("Hey, maybe there's something we both did in high school that we have in common. Did you play an instrument?") and the telling of the stories ("Yeah, I was the skinny kid who played the tuba that was way too big for him. Our band was really good, though; we actually went to state a couple times.") that affinity is built. And, finding out things you don't have in common with people is just as important as learning of commonalities. The pyramid simply gives you the basis for starting conversations.

In terms of rating the intensity of affinities, the "scoring" of the pyramid would start with a 1 on the bottom level and end with a 5 on the top level. In other words, the higher you move on the pyramid, the stronger the bond would be around the experience at that level (because fewer people share the same experience).

Here's another example (taken from an actual 4-person group of co-workers to whom I assigned this exercise). I often use a 4-level pyramid for training, in order to allow more success at filling in every level.

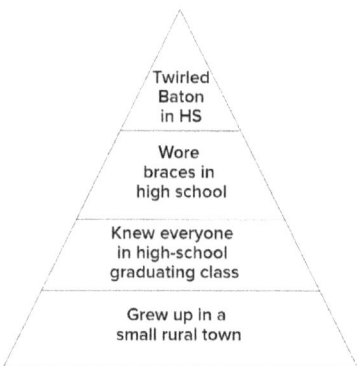

I love to listen to the conversations that take place in the small groups who are working to complete this pyramid exercise. It's especially effective with group members who don't know each other very well.

## It's lonely at the top

It's fun to find exclusive group members on the top of the pyramid with you. But, as you move higher up the pyramid and the affinity score increases, the number of people on each level of the pyramid subsequently decreases. Therefore, people who have very unique life experiences are often alone or nearly alone at the top of the pyramid. Maybe you're the only CEO your company has ever had; maybe you're one of few women in your community with a stay-at-home-husband; maybe you're the only woman in your office currently breastfeeding and needing to use your pump at the office; maybe you're the only man at your company who is a cancer survivor. What can you do to make it less lonely at the top of these pyramids? Realize this: you may be focusing too much on that top level of the affinity pyramid. Yes, you may be the only woman in your office who is currently a nursing mother. You may feel like nobody can relate and that there's no one to talk to about it. Direct your focus to the next couple levels down in the pyramid. There are plenty of women, albeit not currently at your office, who are holding down successful careers while being nursing mothers. Join an internet chat or support group; follow blogs about the topic, reach out to women on-line.

And, for you men who are still reading this chapter even after seeing the word *breastfeeding* ... I applaud you. Your first thought may be that this particular pyramid is totally irrelevant to you. If you're thinking outside the box (or outside the pyramid, as the case may be), you may have already thought of the fact that there are other times in your life when you may have been alone at the top of a similar affinity pyramid. It may involve being the only one in your office at a particular phase in your life who is going through something challenging. Maybe you were once the guy who had to leave early every day to check in on his elderly mother. Maybe you were the man whose wife was pregnant and calling you three times a day. Get the point?

There will be times in all of our lives when we feel we are nearly alone on the top of the pyramid. Just as in any other type of affinity building, we need to be *intentional* about finding others who are sharing or have experienced the same things (or at least similar things) we're going through. The electronic culture allows us to read about others' life challenges and joys. We can then take it further and reach out to people personally.

## A call to action

You saw the various action items located throughout the book. These actions are also listed at the end of the book so you can refer back to them and be intentional about incorporating them into your affinity-building journey.

If you're leading a team, here are a couple ideas for continuing the learning this book started:

1. **MEETING AGENDA ITEM:** Add a weekly/monthly two-minute agenda item to your team meetings. Call it something like "Affinity Building Action." Call upon someone to give a brief example of how they implemented one of the action items and how they used it to build affinity and a stronger relationship.

For example, Lydia reported that she hadn't planned on going to her friend's dad's funeral the previous weekend, but she had just read this book and realized attending the funeral showed her love and affinity for her friend better than only sending a card or posting a sympathy note on Facebook. Lydia said, "I'm not big into funerals; they usually give me the creeps. But, I decided to attend this one because I realized it would mean a lot to my friend Tina. Turns out I was one of her only friends that actually stayed for the mass. Tina told me yesterday how much it meant to her just to see me sitting in the church. And another cool thing is that I met one of her cousins that turned out to be a friend of my brother from college. Small world."

2. **AFFINITY ACTION DISCUSSION**: Post the "33 Actions" list in your meeting room or electronic bulletin board. Each week/month, feature one of the action items and encourage team members to share e-mails, internal communications, or Facebook posts about how the action strengthened a relationship or led to further understanding or conversation.

An example of feedback you could receive from a team member:

"A lady came up to me at Six Flags this weekend and asked if I worked at Cedar Ridge Nursing Home (I was wearing my Cedar Ridge polo shirt from this summer's golf outing). When I told her I was a CNA there, she said, 'Bless your heart! My mom was a resident there 10 years ago and got the best care ever! We bought a pool table for your rec room in her memory after she passed because she loved playing pool.' I told her how the residents still love playing pool on that table and that we had actually started a Pool Sharks League. We had a great chat while we waited in the roller coaster line. Cool experience."

Your follow-up could include something like:

"We should post a pic on the Cedar Ridge Facebook page of some of our residents playing pool. We can remind everyone that the table was purchased in the memory of one of our residents. Did you by any chance get this lady's name?"

"Cool idea. Yes, she gave me her business card. I'll look to see if she has a Facebook page, and we could even tag her in the post."

Needless to say, the initial conversation started because a team member was practicing Action #22, which led to a really neat relationship-building opportunity. Not only will the follow up photo on Facebook pay homage to the beloved former resident and her family, but it will also perhaps inspire other families to think about how they can honor their parents' memories with practical gifts to the community. On and on goes the ripple effect of one small interaction that was followed through with intention.

So that you have all 33 action ideas in one spot, here's a list. I add to the list regularly, and I hope you will, too.

---

## 33 AFFINITY-BUILDING ACTIONS

1. Ask questions.
2. Share your stories with friends, family, and strangers.
3. Acquire a taste for something that is out of your comfort zone.
4. Smile!
5. When you introduce yourself to someone new, use both your first and last name.

6. Use "we" more than "I."
7. Spread the word. Pass along good information and advice to others.
8. Include a unique personal fact on your bio.
9. When breaking the ice with a new group, ask an open-ended question about the past.
10. Promote a "Word of the Week" in your home or workplace.
11. Send cards.
12. When introducing people to each other, mention something they have in common.
13. Be a good audience member; make eye contact with the speaker and nod to show understanding.
14. Follow up promptly after meeting someone new by sending a note that mentions something that brought them to mind that week.
15. Recognize and embrace the positive similarities you have with your parents.
16. Join a support group.
17. Experience things live and in real time.
18. Look for examples of affinity building in books, movies, and everyday interactions.
19. Play interactive games that require conversation and creative communication.
20. Talk to strangers.
21. Go to weddings and funerals. Don't skip the wedding ceremony; stay for the funeral luncheon.
22. Wear logo apparel.
23. Participate in a Community Book Read.
24. Use figures of speech.
25. Pay genuine compliments every day.
26. Go to garage/estate/tag sales.
27. When you host a party, give it a title and theme.
28. Go to all of your class reunions.

29. Utilize social media to its fullest. Be intentional, personal, and generous.
30. Share embarrassing moments.
31. Personalize your Happy Birthday wishes.
32. Create a family mission statement.
33. Join a club.

And, finally, let me know you read this book! I'd so appreciate it if you'd go to my book's Facebook page (Seeking Common Bonds) and tell me one thing you've done or will do differently as a result of reading this book.

My sincere best wishes to you as you seek to become an intentional affinity-builder!

To learn more about Affinity Building Workshops, visit www.buildaffinity.com. I'd love to help you and/or your work, sports, or volunteer team become intentional affinity-builders!